MW00445253

Mona,

Build it up!

Owen

June 2013

Six Sigma Green Belt, Round 2

Also available from ASQ Quality Press:

Lean-Six Sigma for the Public Sector: Leveraging Continuous Process Improvement to Build Better Governments
Brandon Cole

Office Kaizen 2: Harnessing Leadership, Organizations, People, and Tools for Office Excellence
William Lareau

Lean for Service Organizations and Offices: A Holistic Approach for Achieving Operational Excellence and Improvements
Debashis Sarkar

The Executive Guide to Understanding and Implementing Lean Six Sigma: The Financial Impact
Robert M. Meisel, Steven J. Babb, Steven F. Marsh, and James P. Schlichting

Six Sigma for the New Millennium: A CSSBB Guidebook, Second Edition
Kim H. Pries

5S for Service Organizations and Offices: A Lean Look at Improvements
Debashis Sarkar

The Certified Six Sigma Black Belt Handbook, Second Edition
T. M. Kubiak and Donald W. Benbow

The Certified Six Sigma Green Belt Handbook
Roderick A. Munro, Matthew J. Maio, Mohamed B. Nawaz, Govindarajan Ramu, and Daniel J. Zrymiak

The Certified Six Sigma Master Black Belt Handbook
T. M. Kubiak

The Quality Toolbox, Second Edition
Nancy R. Tague

Mapping Work Processes, Second Edition
Bjørn Andersen, Tom Fagerhaug, Bjørnar Henriksen, and Lars E. Onsøyen

Root Cause Analysis: Simplified Tools and Techniques, Second Edition
Bjørn Andersen and Tom Fagerhaug

Lean ISO 9001: Adding Spark to your ISO 9001 QMS and Sustainability to your Lean Efforts
Mike Micklewright

Root Cause Analysis: The Core of Problem Solving and Corrective Action
Duke Okes

To request a complimentary catalog of ASQ Quality Press publications, call 800-248-1946, or visit our Web site at http://www.asq.org/quality-press.

Six Sigma Green Belt, Round 2

Making Your Next Project Better Than the Last One

Tracy L. Owens

ASQ Quality Press
Milwaukee, Wisconsin

American Society for Quality, Quality Press, Milwaukee 53203
© 2012 by ASQ
All rights reserved. Published 2011
Printed in the United States of America
17 16 15 14 13 12 11   5 4 3 2 1

Library of Congress Cataloging-in-Publication Data

Owens, Tracy L.
  Six Sigma green belt, round 2 : making your next project better than the last one /
Tracy L. Owens.
     p. cm.
  Includes bibliographical references and index.
  ISBN 978-0-87389-825-6 (hard cover : alk. paper)
  1. Six sigma (Quality control standard) 2. Quality control—Management. 3. Cost.
I. Title.

HD62.15.O924 2011
658.4'013—dc23   2011027385

ISBN: 978-0-87389-825-6

No part of this book may be reproduced in any form or by any means, electronic,
mechanical, photocopying, recording, or otherwise, without the prior written permission
of the publisher.

Publisher: William A. Tony
Acquisitions Editor: Matt T. Meinholz
Project Editor: Paul O'Mara
Production Administrator: Randall Benson

ASQ Mission: The American Society for Quality advances individual, organizational,
and community excellence worldwide through learning, quality improvement, and
knowledge exchange.

Attention Bookstores, Wholesalers, Schools, and Corporations: ASQ Quality Press
books, video, audio, and software are available at quantity discounts with bulk
purchases for business, educational, or instructional use. For information, please
contact ASQ Quality Press at 800-248-1946, or write to ASQ Quality Press,
P.O. Box 3005, Milwaukee, WI 53201-3005.

To place orders or to request ASQ membership information, call 800-248-1946. Visit our
website at http://www.asq.org/quality-press.

 Printed on acid-free paper

 Quality Press
600 N. Plankinton Ave.
Milwaukee, WI 53203-2914
E-mail: authors@asq.org

ASQ **The Global Voice of Quality™**

Table of Contents

Part VI   Overall Business Process Management

CD-ROM Contents

Tools and Templates	File Names
Cause and Effects Matrix	CE matrix.xls
Communication Plan	Communication Plan template.doc
Control Charts	control-chart.xls
Control/Response Plan	ControlResponsePlan.ppt ControlResponsePlan.xls
Cost–Benefit Analysis	Simple Cost Benefit Analysis.xlsx
Data Collection Plan	Data Collection Plan.xlsx
Fishbone Diagram	fishbone-cause-and-effect-diagram.xls fishbone blank.ppt
Flowcharts	flow-chart-template.xls
Graphs	box-and-whisker-plot.xls Pareto-chart.xls scatter-diagram.xls Time Series Plot sample.xls
Hypothesis Tests—T-Test	Paired_t_and_F_test.xls
Regression	Linear Regression Analysis.xlsx
Chi-Squared	Chi_Square.xls,
Measurement System Analysis	MSA GRR form.xls
Process FMEA	FMEA-Sample.xls
Project Charter	Charter template.doc
Scope Contract	ScopeContractTemplate.ppt
SIPOC and Value-Add/Non-Value-Add Analysis	SIPOC and VA-NVA template.xls
Stakeholder Analysis and Influence Strategy	Stakeholder Analysis template.doc

List of Figures and Tables

Preface

The Green Belt has been embraced by many organizations as a very effective resource in pursuit of lower operating costs, higher productivity, better customer service, less waste, and faster processes. As a practitioner of lean and Six Sigma, the Green Belt executes projects that bring tangible savings to the organization. The Green Belt often experiences a renewed sense of employee engagement, as do those who participate on a project team or whose processes are being improved. Equally impressive has been the increase in effectiveness of those who have been selected to become Green Belts. They usually emerge from the program with better business acumen, new tools in their toolboxes, stronger professional contacts, and greater respect from their organizations.

Typical Green Belt programs involve a one- or two-week training class, a proficiency test on the topics that were covered during training, and execution of one project that follows the Six Sigma methodology. This is a good plan: to learn the material, prove that you've learned it, and apply it to a real situation. After that, though, the Green Belts may get less attention and may be expected to lead another project with less active coaching than they had during their first projects. This can be challenging since most projects are not exactly the same as any previous project. The process will be different, the variables will be different, the solutions needed will be different. So, translating the knowledge gained by the Green Belt during project number one may not be easy for the next project.

This is the aim of this book: to make your next project better than the last one. If you've completed one Six Sigma project—congratulations! Now, let's get you back in the ring to make more improvements. If you have never led such a project, the material in this book will also help you to get started and to complete a useful project in a manageable period of time. In ninety days you can improve your process by defining the need clearly, involving the right people, conducting a thorough study, making sound decisions based on facts, testing your solution, and institutionalizing the improvement. That will be your goal: a good project that is completed in ninety days.

As a parallel outline with the popular and effective DMAIC methodology, Chapters 1 and 2 include elements commonly found in the *define* phase of an improvement project, Chapters 3 and 4—*measure*, Chapters 5 and 6—*analyze*, Chapters 7 and 8—*improve*, and Chapter 9—*control*. Chapter 10 concerns overall business process management and can be used any time, whether you're leading a project or not.

Techniques from lean enterprise will also be very useful in managing a good project in a short period of time. Lean tools will be used primarily in the early stages of the project, including value stream mapping and identifying quick wins, the *improve* phase of the project when increasing efficiency and removing waste, and in ongoing process management, which is discussed in the final chapter.

There is always more to say on all these subjects, and there are volumes and volumes of material on every topic in this book. The author's intention is to help you begin making improvements today.

Let's get started!

Introduction

In the thirteen years since I began my formal education in process improvement, I have heard a lot of praise for the Lean Six Sigma approach. Organizations of all sizes are saving real money, improving their customer service, and developing talented managers from within their teams. Whether the approach is called continuous improvement, process excellence, business transformation, or something else, a focused effort on improving critical processes throughout the organization using Six Sigma, lean, and other useful tools is driving tangible benefits all around the world.

Often, the initiative will take hold in one area of the organization and grow from there. Perhaps one or two motivated leaders explore the possibilities and prove that the program works by executing a few successful projects. Very often, an organization will commission a staff of professionals—Six Sigma Black Belts—to take the lead, find and execute projects, and calculate the savings. These experts in process improvement pay for themselves very quickly and become important leaders in the organization. Whether they report to finance, operations, supply chain, or anywhere else, their reach is broad, and the savings they achieve are real.

I have also occasionally heard a complaint about Six Sigma. In the eyes of business managers, who have a responsibility to produce results for their stakeholders, the complaint is that Six Sigma projects take too long to complete and to realize financial savings or a positive impact on the customer. A year after the kickoff meeting, the team is still telling the executive steering committee that they're working on it. Unknown problems arise, team members get promoted to another area or quit, the project fizzles, and the project leader grasps for even the smallest amount of financial benefit before closing the file with a sigh of relief.

In very successful organizations a tipping point is reached, and the separate group of Black Belts is no longer the main instrument of the improvement efforts. Instead, the staff at large becomes interested in driving improvements in areas not previously touched by the Six Sigma group, and they seek training opportunities and conduct projects that were not on the continuous improvement program's master project list. This is a very powerful moment in time. People all around the organization will learn to use the tools and techniques, and then they will apply them during the course of performing their jobs, not as an additional duty. They will start to generate enthusiasm, savings, and talent that are far beyond any expectations that were set during strategic planning sessions and budget reviews—kicking into high gear, you might say. These talented people are the Green Belts—people who continue to work their jobs, just at a higher level of proficiency using the lean and Six Sigma suite of tools they have been trained on. That is the group this book is intended to reach.

With the material in this book—tools, templates, and techniques—we can also defeat the problem of projects taking too long. It will be overcome by following the steps outlined in the first nine chapters when conducting any project. Tables I.1 and I.2 outline the timeline for completing a project in ninety days and the nine essential requirements for a succesful project. This road map for project success will offer the project leader the elements of a positive foundation: achievable project goals, objective decision-making criteria, proven causes of the problem, and a chance to prove that the solution works. You have the skill in yourself and your team to accomplish all the objectives set forth in your improvement project charter. It is within your power to improve your process, and to do it quickly. Prescribed throughout the chapters is a series of meetings choreographed for the Green Belt project leader and team to help achieve the desired objectives and keep pace with the goal of ninety days for project completion. I have rarely encountered a person who would argue that a project that was successfully completed in ninety days took too long to execute.

Table I.1 Proposed project timeline.

Before day one	The team is formed: two to seven core team members and any additional subject matter experts to help when needed. Team leader and project sponsor collaborate on initial project charter.
Day one	Kickoff meeting to establish teamwork, complete project charter, and begin mapping the process that will be improved.
First week	Team leader revises charter with project sponsor. Team finishes process maps and reviews them with process owners and operators. Look for quick wins!
Second week	Second team meeting to review finished process maps. Data collection begins following discussion of process variables.
Weeks three through five	Monitor data collection to be sure everybody is conducting it according to plan.
Week six	Team meeting to review data collection. Cause-and-effect (fishbone) analysis takes place. Team will identify possible root causes for defects, variation, and other problems. Look for quick wins! Data collection continues.
Weeks seven through nine	Data collection continues. Team leader tests validity of root causes using statistical, graphical, and process analysis.
Weeks ten through twelve	Team meets to develop solutions. Team prepares and executes pilot test. Refinements of solutions are made following testing. Team leader creates initial draft of control/response plan.
Day ninety	Final team meeting to implement updated process, institute control/response plan, and celebrate success!

Table I.2 The nine essential project requirements and accompanying tools.

1. Clearly defined scope	Project charter, scope contract
2. Process maps	Flowcharts, VA/NVA
3. Sufficient data	Data collection plan
4. Consistent measurement	Measurement system analysis
5. List of possible causes	Fishbone diagram, cause-and-effect matrix
6. Verified root causes	Hypothesis test, graphs
7. Pilot test	Influence strategy, FMEA
8. Cost–benefit analysis	CBA template
9. Control/response plan	Communication plan, control charts

Throughout the book we will discuss ways to make projects better. The benefits of following these steps and the reasons for taking them will be explained. It will be useful in places to give examples of how *not* following these steps can be detrimental. Some of the stories may ring very true to you. All the names have been changed to protect the innocent!

Part I

Define

1

Clearly Defined Scope

There are many reasons why improvement projects take too long to execute. Of course, even the definition of "too long" can vary from one person to another, and the variation between two people's expectations for the duration of a project is a problem in itself. We resolve that problem at the very beginning by setting a timeline and agreeing to it. If we use the timeline presented in the Introduction, we're looking at about a ninety-day project. How long did your first project take?

One of the primary reasons for unexpectedly long projects is the inflated amount of achievement the project is expected to undertake; the scope of the project is often just too large. To set a broad objective for a project team, such as *improve customer service*, *reduce defective parts*, or *increase on-time delivery*, is to set the team up for failure. These are important objectives, of course. The problem is that they are not specific about how to improve, what details to improve, or even how much improvement is expected. In addition, project objectives like *update the training manual*, *implement the new ERP system*, or *clean the factory* are not even process improvement projects at all.

IN ORDER TO IMPROVE THE PROCESS, THERE MUST BE A PROCESS

Initiating a process improvement project first requires that a few questions can be answered with a "yes":

- Is there a documented or understood process in place?

- Are the people who are expected to follow the process doing so every time?

- Is the process failing to produce the desired results?

Let's look at these questions individually and in the sequence presented.

Question #1: Is there a documented or understood process in place? If there is not a process in place, it is not really possible to improve the process. If there is no stated expectation, then no one can be held to any standard. For example, if there are six underwriters at an insurance company and each conducts the investigation of a similar risk in different ways, how can you know which process is best?

- If one spends a lot of time in order to make the best decision, could the process have been done faster?

The three scenarios listed here illustrate the potential conflicts between speed, accuracy, and cost. If you want something done right, it may take time and it may cost money. If you want something done cheaply, there may be delays and defects. If you want something done fast, it may have errors and it may be expensive. You can sometimes achieve two of the three, but the third may be difficult to accomplish. If you want something done quickly, correctly, and frugally, the principles presented in this book can help!

- If another spends money conducting research using various outside sources, could the same conclusion have been drawn using the information the company already owns?

- And if a third makes decisions quickly, yet is only accurate 75% of the time, how much more time or effort would bring that figure closer to 90%, or 95%?

If there is not a process in place, write one so you at least have a place to start. Some methods you can follow to develop a documented process include: studying the work that is being performed and using that as a foundation, benchmarking a similar process being executed at another organization, using Design for Six Sigma to construct a process that will meet the needs of your customers, or following another path that has worked for you or your mentors in the past. Document the process and share your expectation with all your team members. Provide an environment conducive to process execution and excellence, with the necessary tools for the job, and keep an eye on safety and work/life balance. Train the staff to build their skills in completing the work. And motivate the team as needed. It is not a surprise that you and your organization have the desire to improve performance. After all, you have probably completed one or more improvement projects already, which is a testament to your commitment.

If there is a process in place, proceed to question #2.

Question #2: Are the people who are expected to follow the process doing so every time? If the process is not being followed, then we don't even know if it is capable of producing the desired results. For example, a truck fleet determined that it was paying too much for fuel. To reduce its overall fuel cost, the fleet opened an account with a nationwide fuel provider and instructed all drivers that the new process was to use this one source for fuel. The drivers did not comply with these instructions for various reasons: "I know where I can find fuel cheaper," "It costs me the difference in the price of fuel just to drive over to the new provider," and other explanations were given by the drivers when asked why they did not use the identified fuel provider. As a result, the fleet did not learn anything new about its process and was not able to determine whether the account they opened with the new fuel provider gave them a fuel cost savings.

If the established process is not being followed, use this troubleshooter:

1. Have you clearly communicated your expectation to the team that the process must be followed?

2. Are you providing an environment where success is possible? Or are there obstacles in the way that prevent following the process?

3. Have you provided the necessary skill training to your team?

4. If you feel you have been successful in all of these areas, and your team agrees, then you must ask whether the team is motivated to perform.

The answers to these troubleshooting questions can be very illuminating. Resolve the issues, get your team to follow the established process, and then proceed to the next question.

PROJECT CHARTER

Question #3: Is the process failing to produce the desired results? If the process is failing to achieve the necessary results, an improvement project is needed. To run a good project, some basic instructions need to be outlined at the beginning. First of all, you must identify the specific problem and memorialize it. Today's problem will be history in ninety days, and you will want to show how much improvement you have made. This first item will be known as the *problem statement.* It is a clear expression of the failures of the process as it exists today. It is quantifiable and specific. A good way to quantify problems is to choose which of these important areas is most impacted: speed, accuracy, or cost:

- Is today's problem that the process takes too long or that the results are not delivered on time? This is a speed problem.

- Is the issue that defects are being produced and some of them have to be fixed before they reach the customer, or some of them actually do reach the customer? These are accuracy issues, and they are often quantified with a defect rate or a *yield,* which is the percent that are done correctly at every step of the process.

- Or is the problem that the process costs too much to execute?

These are three main ways to spot and quantify today's problems in your process. Examples of problem statements are shown in Table 1.1.

Table 1.1   Examples of problem statements.

Unclear problem statement	Better problem statement
Our customers are not satisfied with our product	Customer satisfaction with PKR product quality was rated 63% last quarter, an all-time low
Product delivery is slower than expected	On-time delivery of D-pipes is 87%: 11% are late, and 2% are too early for customers to use
Transaction fees are too high	Payments made via electronic data interchange (EDI) cost 1.5 times the budget for accounts in the western United States

Next, the team who executes this project must know what the desired outcome is. The process is broken today. What will it look like when it is fixed? We'll answer this question in the *goal statement*, which is also quantifiable and specific. Examples of goal statements related to the "better" problem statements in Table 1.1 are shown in Table 1.2.

How much of an improvement is a good goal, by the way? There are many possible ways to answer this question. Here are three:

- If the process is producing 10% or fewer failures, set a goal to improve it by 50%.

- If the process is producing more than 10% defects, target an improvement of 90%.

- Set a goal that is slightly better than an industry benchmark.

These goal-setting standards are designed to help your team achieve a goal that is realistic. Goals such as "we will never create a defective part" or "we will arrive exactly 20 minutes early on 100% of our deliveries" may be unachievable and unrealistic and may give the team the feeling that any improvement they make that is short of 100 percent will not be good enough.

The next instruction to record at the beginning of the project is the set of *roles and responsibilities* for the members of the team. Identifying by name the team's members, the project leader, the organizational leader who is responsible for the performance of the process (commonly called the *project sponsor*), and any subject matter experts who will be needed on occasion to add important information to the team's work and discussions will make it clear to the team and the entire organization exactly who is involved and how much of their time will be required over the next ninety days.

Another tactical element of the project instructions will be the timeline, or *project plan*. It could be as simple as

Today—Start

Ninety days from today—End

although a little more detail would be helpful to the organizational leaders who may want to check the team's progress.

Table 1.2   Examples of goal statements.

Unclear goal statement	Better goal statement
Improve customer satisfaction	Improve product quality so that customer satisfaction scores return to the previous level of 83% or higher by the end of Q3
Improve on-time delivery	By the end of June, reduce variation in delivery time for D-pipes so at least 97% are delivered within the specified window of time
Reduce transaction fees	Bring EDI charges back within budget by November 30

A road map of your project plan could look like this:

March 1—Kickoff meeting

March 8—Working meeting, begin data collection

April 12—Team meeting, review data

May 10—Team meeting, analyze data, and prepare improvement plan

May 11 to 24—Pilot test and refine process

May 24—Documentation and closure meeting

Advantages of a specified project calendar include: reserved calendar space for team members, awareness of the meeting dates for senior leaders who will want to check progress, and a sense of urgency about completing assignments between meetings. A ninety-day project requires commitment from all team members.

The document where all these instructions are recorded is the *project charter*. The charter is shared widely because the improvement project is not a secret. If it is not shared, then people will not know that an effort is being made to improve a broken process, the same work could be duplicated elsewhere in the organization unnecessarily, the team members will be pulled to other tasks, and the other leaders in the organization will not be able to track the progress of the project. It is important to note that changing the charter after the project begins is permissible, if necessary. If assumptions don't match reality, if a goal needs to be adjusted, or if a scheduled meeting or a team member's name must be changed, then an updated (and dated) charter should be published.

CONFIRMING THE PROJECT SCOPE

There are two more critical elements of the project charter. One is the *scope* of the project. The discussion of scope includes a few items such as the size of the objective, as discussed earlier in this chapter. A great way to keep projects short in duration is to keep them narrow in scope. Rather than assigning one overly large project to a huge team, break that project into pieces corresponding to the process and improve the individual sections. A factory that molds plastic parts was suffering a high reject rate from its customers. Instead of demanding "Improve our parts!" of his staff, the plant manager broke the problem down into the types of defects that were being discovered: cracks in parts, discoloration, black specks or spots, and splay or spiderwebs in the plastic. With separate teams working on each defect type and comparing notes, they were able to reduce the amount of rejected parts from two garbage bags full to one sandwich bag full in less than three months!

Scope also includes the areas of the organization that will and will not be examined for improvement opportunities in pursuit of overall problem resolution. It may not be possible to change the location of the presses or the computer system that is in place, so those items would be listed on the charter as out of scope. Further, the scope also includes the start and end points of the process that is being improved. If the overall process is depicted in a flowchart, then the part of the process that the team is seeking to improve must be visible somewhere specific in the overall flow. In the case shown in Figure 1.1, the process for completing investigation of a special type of loan has been identified as a problem, so only that part of the overall process is included in the scope of the improvement project.

The decision on which part or parts of the process to improve is generated from the answer to an earlier question: Is the process failing to produce the desired results? The results that are missing the objective are generated somewhere in the overall process. If the defects are created in multiple locations in the process, remember to start specific improvement projects to address each problem, thereby not initiating a project that can not be completed in ninety days.

In addition to the project charter, a written tool that has been very helpful to improvement project managers is the *scope contract* (see Figure 1.2).

At the beginning of the project, the project leader prepares the scope contract with the team's help. The contract details the items that the project scope comprises: the specific process that will be addressed, start and end points of the process, and the functions

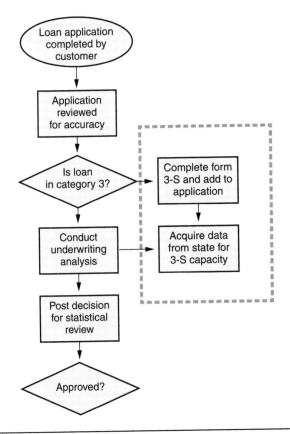

Figure 1.1   Flowchart with specific problem area identified.

Project name: Improve Speed of Admissions	Start date: November 30, 2011	Expected completion: February 24, 2012
Process *starts* with first referral call	*In scope:*	*Out of scope:*
Process *ends* at in-processing interview	Scheduling of staff, paper-based data collection versus database, sequence of events prior to admission, current reporting requirements.	Changes to current automated systems are not in scope. Clinical review process must be completed prior to admission.
	As additional questions arise on what is "in scope," team leader will consult with project sponsor as quickly as possible.	Risks of adding more to scope of the project are an extended timeline and a delay in implementing solutions.
	Project leader signature	Project sponsor signature

Figure 1.2   Completed sample scope contract.

that are in and out of scope. The scope contract is then agreed to and signed by the project's sponsor. An example of the effectiveness of a scope contract is the project started by a Green Belt in 2003 to improve the controls at a financial services company based on the Sarbanes-Oxley legislation. When he and his project sponsor met to outline his responsibilities, they agreed that he would handle only four areas of the business in order to make sure they were ready by the parent company's deadline. Two weeks later, the sponsor asked the Green Belt to add a fifth area of the business to the scope of his project. The Green Belt referred to the original agreement, detailed the amount of work that was being conducted by him and his small team, and realistically estimated that the deadline would be missed by five days if the additional work were included. The sponsor accepted his assessment and started another small group to work in parallel with the Green Belt's team, with both teams sharing knowledge. All five areas that needed improvement were completed on time, which was good for the business. What was even better for the Green Belt was that, despite his initial hesitation at saying no to the high-ranking business leader who asked him to add to the initial project, he and the project sponsor continued to work on many more projects after that time, and the Green Belt was later offered a job leading one of the functions in his department by the sponsor.

The sixth element of the project charter, usually listed first, is the *business case*. The business case answers these questions:

- Why should we conduct this project now?

- How does this process improvement help the organization toward achieving its goals?

- What is the risk of not making this improvement?

Table 1.3   Examples of business cases.

Unclear business case	Better business case
Customer satisfaction is important, so we should improve it	Customer satisfaction with PKR is important because the competitor's product has gained market share over the past three quarters
Late deliveries are viewed negatively by our customers	On-time delivery is a competitive advantage for us considering the complexity of the assembled products
When fees are too high, we make less money	Missing the budget for EDI may limit our ability to expand its use into receivables collection, which is expected to save the company $3.4 million per year when implemented

Examples of business case statements are shown in Table 1.3.

When the charter is prepared, it should be a comprehensive record of the project's starting point. It includes the who, what, when, where, and why of the improvement that is required. It should serve as a useful reference when questions arise later, or especially when the scope begins to creep into other areas.

An effective response to *scope creep* is to spin off a new project. Hidden problems often emerge during the course of an improvement study, and it can be tempting to add them to your objective. Not only will that add time to your project, it can also prevent the growth of skills in project leadership and process improvement among your team members. It is often true that today's project team member will want to be tomorrow's project leader. What better development opportunity is there than to spin off a new, chartered project that a member of the existing project team can lead next? With the right coaching, a team member who has the aptitude and interest in project leadership can turn into yet another resource for your organization when the need for improvement next arises.

2

Process Maps

Take a minute and draw on a piece of paper your process for collecting voice mail. Office phone, mobile phone, home phone—any phone is fine for this exercise. When you are finished, you may have something like this:

1. Written:

    a. See the blinking light

    b. Lift the handset

    c. Push the "voice mail" button

    d. Listen to each message

    e. Save messages I need for later

    f. Erase all other messages

    g. End call

    h. Return urgent calls immediately

2. Picture:

1	2	3
4	5	6
7	8	9
★	0	#

Enter code, push 1 to listen, push 2 to erase, push 3 to save, push * to disconnect

3. Flowchart:

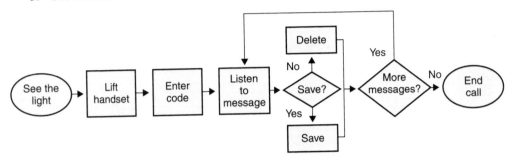

None of these is wrong, even though the instruction was to *draw* your process. Any representation of the process that helps you understand the steps that need to be taken is fine. The question you are going to ask is, "Will this set of notes, picture, or flowchart help somebody else understand how to perform this process, just in case I'm not able to do it myself?"

IMPORTANCE OF PROCESS MAPS

Process maps really pave the way to success in a project. Everything the team does throughout the project will tie back to the process maps, and, in the end, a new process map will be created to reflect the updated, improved process. The primary importance of the process map is that it establishes a baseline understanding of the process and the way it works today. That will give the team a consistent view of the variation and difficulties that the operators of the process are facing. Further, the team will have a visual representation of the process from which they can identify inconsistencies and uncover quick wins early in the project.

The process map really leads into all other elements of the project, and it is specifically tied to these:

- Identifying the variables that the data collection plan will comprise (Chapter 3)

- Guiding the fishbone diagram discussions (Chapter 5)

- Testing for root causes of the problems and variation (Chapter 6)

- Serving as the foundation for the failure modes and effects analysis (Chapter 7)

- Providing the basis for pilot testing a new solution (Chapter 7)

- Developing the control/response plan (Chapter 9)

Taking a lesson from the previous chapter, if someone wanted to convince you that process mapping is a good idea, then the next question must be asked: What is the risk of not making a map of the process?

Answer: Starting a project without mapping the process that is being improved can lead to confusion about the start and end points of the targeted process, disagreement about the scope of the project, unclear understanding of the steps in the process, inaccurate assumptions about the process because it has not been verified with the actual operators, improvements that do not have a positive effect on the outcome of the process, and significant delays in project completion.

HOW TO CREATE PROCESS MAPS

Diagramming of voice mail collection can turn out differently in a group of people. It will probably still be understood, since gathering voice mail is pretty familiar to most people by now. For more sophisticated processes, or processes that are being seen and executed for the first time by a new person, it will be helpful to draw the diagram with some common process mapping symbols. Figure 2.1 depicts a few that are frequently used.

When mapping the process, start with an oval at the point where the process begins. The next step in the process is added as a box with an arrow connecting the two. If the next step in the process requires a decision to be made, that is represented with a diamond asking the question (see Figure 2.2), and it is followed by two arrows: one for the trail that will be followed if the answer is *yes*, and one for *no* (see Figure 2.3).

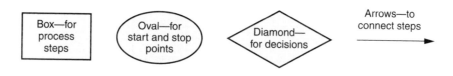

Figure 2.1   Common process mapping symbols.

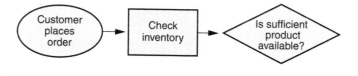

Figure 2.2   First steps in process mapping.

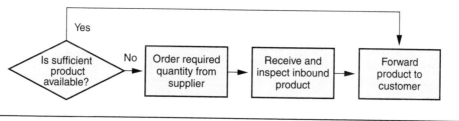

Figure 2.3   Representing decision points in a process map.

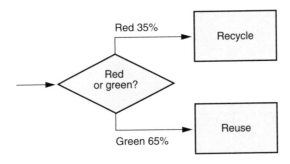

Figure 2.4   Alternate method of representing decision points in a process map.

If other choices besides *yes* and *no* are appropriate, they can be used in the process map. A variation in the use of decision boxes is to add the percentage of time that each path is usually taken. This can provide more information on the process that can be used to improve it (see Figure 2.4).

The symbols presented here are the most commonly used, but there are many more types of boxes and connectors available if such a level of detail is required. The symbols you choose really only need to accomplish one objective: to make sure that everyone understands the depiction of the process. Even if you decide to invent a new symbol that is specific to a process step that your organization uses, that is fine as long as everyone knows exactly what it means.

SIPOC: A FLOWCHART WITH WINGS

A wider view of the process can be achieved by mapping your process in the SIPOC format (the letters stand for *suppliers, inputs, process steps, outputs,* and *customers*). In addition to the steps conducted in the process, the SIPOC chart also includes information that can help your team to identify possible problems and sources of variation. The term SIPOC reflects the left-to-right elements that the diagram comprises. Since one of the strengths of a Six Sigma program is that the projects all begin by studying and detailing that which is important to the customer, let me explain the terms in reverse order.

- *Customers.* These are the people who will receive the results of your process step. At the end of the overall process being performed, the "customer" will be the actual end customer who is buying your product or service. The customer at the end of the process can also include regulatory authorities, financial analysts, and others who depend on your process to do their work. During the overall process, the "customer" could be the next department or team in your organization to be involved in the process. When you think of downstream people in your organization as customers, you may be able to provide them with better inputs to their process steps.

- *Outputs.* These are the results of the process *step* that is being conducted, not the output of the overall process. If at one point in the overall process there is a process step to add rivets to a sheet of aluminum, the output of that process step is a riveted sheet. This is important because it is the necessary input for the next process step.

- *Process steps.* A process step is the activity in the process that is currently being conducted. In the example in Figure 2.5, there are seven steps that the order entry agent must perform once the order is sent. For each of those process steps, there is a set of inputs and a set of outputs. Every step in the process must be analyzed in this way to find the causes of defects and variation. *If a step in the process is analyzed and found to provide no significant output that is important to any internal or external customer, then that process step really needs to be considered for elimination.*

- *Inputs.* These include whatever is brought into the process step in order to produce the necessary output, including materials, labor, information, parts, output from previous steps, and anything else that the operator or process owner needs in order to do the job.

- *Suppliers.* These are the people, departments, vendors, or other functions that provide the tools you need to do the job, including instructions, information, and raw materials—in short, everything that is in the "Inputs" column in Figure 2.5.

In addition to the facts that you will find during the comprehensive study of the process steps depicted in the P column of the SIPOC chart, it is very possible that the items listed in the S, I, O, and C columns could be contributing to the problems in your process. You might study the output of your process and find that all the late deliveries included raw materials supplied by a specific vendor, or that all outputs of a specific type at a certain step in your process need to be reworked. As an example, one insurance company found that a large proportion of the mistakes that had been made in rate changes were found in two specific geographic regions. This was useful information because it led to the discovery of a programming error that had been made three years earlier and not caught at that time.

The SIPOC chart is also a very good tool for guiding a conversation with the project team at the beginning of the project. The team will leave this session with a much better understanding of the process that is going to be improved and the critical elements that make that process successful.

VALUE STREAM MAPPING

Taking process mapping to the next level, *value stream mapping* incorporates more details about the business into the drawn diagram.

Suppliers	Inputs	Process steps	Outputs	Customers
Customer's purchasing agent	Purchase order sent via fax, e-mail, or EDI	Order is sent	Legible text and usable format	Order entry staff (customer service)
Customer's purchasing agent	Product codes, quantity, and prices	Confirm order details	Order data ready for entry into system	Backup service reps in case entry is delayed
Our account manager	Current catalog or promotion/special	Valid info?	Pricing revisions, codes for special promotions	Marketing department needs promotion data
Our supply chain function	Table of production schedules by category	Check product availability	Product availability dates	Order entry staff (customer service)
Our production operations	Estimated production or availability	Available?	Estimated ship date for this order	Order entry staff and end customer
Order entry staff	Reserve note template and required data	Prepare reserve note	Reserve note document sent	End customer
Order entry staff	Shipment confirmation template and data	Confirm shipment date	Shipment notification sent	End customer
Our accounts receivable team	Initial invoice template and required data	Prepare initial invoice	Initial invoice sent	End customer

Figure 2.5   Process map in SIPOC format—the order entry part of a customer service function.

Additional symbols are used to show processes that push materials to the next process versus those that pull materials from the previous process only when they are needed, level loading of a work space, manual information flow and electronic information flow, storage locations and the ways that they are used, and even the number of operators engaged in production at each step in the overall process. This is not just a technique that is useful in factories, either. Value stream mapping can be helpful in any work environment where processes convert inputs into outputs over a period of time. A sample value stream map is depicted in Figure 2.6.

The next step in value stream mapping would be to identify a few critical points in the process:

- What is the *pacemaker*? This is the step in the process that dictates the overall time required to complete the full process, and it is usually the closest step in the process to the actual customer. For this reason, scheduling for the overall process really depends on the time required to complete the pacemaker step. For example, if a carpet cleaning business is scheduling its jobs for the day, the pacemaker is the actual cleaning of each customer's floors because the time required for this process is known based on the size of the job. Everything else in the process—paperwork, routing, follow-up—can be scheduled around the actual cleaning time.

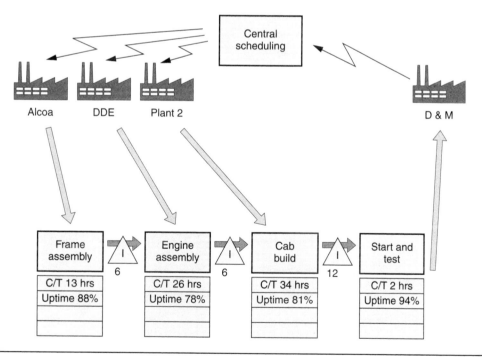

Figure 2.6 Truck assembly process value stream map, in brief. Amount of materials, inventory, orders, and forecasts would be included for planning purposes.

- What process steps that are currently *push* steps could be changed to *pull* steps? (The answer should be—all of them!). *Push* is when you move parts, materials, or information to the next point in the process *before they are needed*. Push creates waste by building up materials and inventory and by sending information that may need to be resent because it was not useful when it was first delivered. *Pull* is waiting for a signal from the next process step that those inputs are needed and then sending them forth.

- What is the time that should be required to complete each task along the process? This is not just a list of historical industrial engineering standards. It is a function that should be calculated based on the pace of order placement by your customers.

The purpose of value stream mapping is to find your sources of waste, eliminate them, and build a new, more efficient process that meets all your customer's needs and does it right the first time. What a great goal for us to have!

You will follow a recommended set of steps for value stream mapping:

1. Walk the process flow yourself, and bring your own stopwatch. Walk the process from front to back, then walk it from back to front. You are looking for the flow of materials and information as a first step toward finding and eliminating waste.

2. Map the value stream yourself, on paper with a pencil. Map the full process, not just parts, and don't divide the work into jobs for separate people. You must get the full view of the value stream.

3. Compare maps with others who have drawn the same value stream, and then present it to the operators and process owners.

4. Look for ways to employ lean techniques.

5. Draw the *future state value stream map* based on how the process could be improved.

6. Develop the plan to achieve that future state and start taking action!

HOW TO USE PROCESS MAPS

At the beginning of Chapter 1, we had to answer three questions in order to know whether a process improvement project should be initiated:

- Is there a process in place?

- Is the process being followed every time?

- Is the process failing to produce the desired results?

Validating the Process Map

After the project team has created the process map or maps, there is an important step to take before using them to start collecting information and identifying improvement opportunities. The team must validate the process map(s) with the actual operators, the people who are performing the process regularly. If the team has drawn a process map that is inaccurate, the risks are serious: you might make corrections to process steps that do not really need to be corrected, you might miss the opportunity to fix a problem because it is not shown on the map, and you could alienate the operators of the process who were not able to contribute to the development of the map. For example, a project team drew a process map for the unloading of baked goods in the forward distribution center. They found that the individual route drivers were supposed to complete their scrap forms while loading the product into their vans and transmit them to the bakery using their handheld devices at that time, which was about 1:30 a.m. each night. So, in order to collect scrap information as quickly as possible, the team added a staff member to the night shift from 10:00 p.m. to 4:00 a.m. in order to collect this information. When that new person did not get any new data for a whole week, the team asked one of the route drivers what was happening. The driver said, "Oh, that's the way it was supposed to work. In reality, we like to start our deliveries as quickly as possible, and we send all the scrap reports after we finish the route." The deliveries were usually finished at about 4:30 a.m.! There was definitely a need to validate the process map with the people who were executing the process.

Process maps are going to help us with each of those answers.

If there is not a process in place and you continued reading this book anyway, then you should get started right away. With the help of your operators, draw a diagram of the steps that are currently being followed so you understand clearly what is being done *today.* You may need more than one diagram if people are performing the steps in different ways. These diagrams will provide a basis from which you can improve and, at least, make the process more consistent in order to study it further. For example, the manager of a ten-person sales team wanted to determine the best way to capture data on sales calls or visits in the customer relationship management database. When she learned that three people entered data at the end of each day from their home computers, three others waited until the end of the week, two stopped into coffee shops for a Wi-Fi connection on most days, one had programmed his handheld device to capture and upload the data, and the tenth sent all his information to a secretary to enter for him, the manager understood why the full set of customer data was not current at any given time during the week.

One end result of mapping an existing process would be a full set of work instructions—even diagrammed or described to the keystroke—necessary in order to accomplish the task. The objective should be that a new operator could perform the task correctly following the process map and instructions on the first day on the job.

For a process that is in place and is not being followed, use the process map to display the appropriate steps. Then review the map thoroughly with the team. Uncover the arguments, hesitation, and causes of resistance with your team and resolve them so that the process can be followed every time. This discussion may even result in changes to a process that you've only recently documented. If this is the case, examine the possibility of incorporating the changes, make sure they will work and will not produce any unintended consequences, and implement them. This exercise in itself can be very motivational, as your team will see proof of their empowerment and of your willingness to involve them in shaping the future of the department. For example, when an accounts payable team was invited to prepare the process maps for their own area, they included a very revealing box that read "Wait for manager to get out of a meeting and approve the form." It didn't take long to establish (1) the guidelines for conditions that require the manager's approval and those that do not, and (2) a backup signer.

Already the process map has proven useful, and you haven't even started the improvement project yet!

LONG-, MEDIUM-, AND SHORT-TERM IMPROVEMENTS

In ninety days you can make a lot of positive changes. Let's call ninety days the medium term for this discussion. The *medium-term improvements* will be the goals of your project, recorded in the charter's goal statement. To finish our definitions, the *short-term improvements* will be those that you can find, study, and implement in less than ninety days or, more properly stated, before the project is complete. The *long-term improvements* you identify are likely to take longer than the term of the project to implement fully. The reason for this extra time might be that the improvement in question is out of scope for this project, and, as a result, a new project should be started or spun off from this one. The long-term improvement may also be viewed as a more difficult change requiring the involvement of a different team of people in a concerted effort to effect that change specifically. It is very illuminating to take a process map that looks like Figure 2.7 when mapped by the project team, and then like Figure 2.8 when validated with the larger population of operators, and turn it into a much simpler diagram (Figure 2.9) of how the process should be and could be transformed within the scope of a ninety-day project.

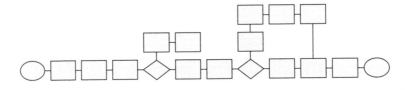

Figure 2.7   Initial, complex process map.

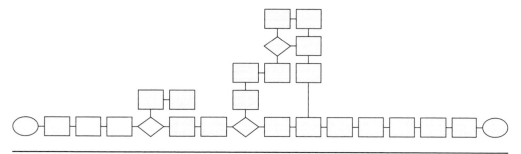

Figure 2.8   Even more complex process map!

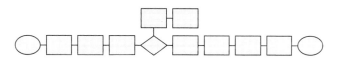

Figure 2.9   Simplified process map.

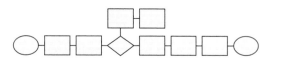

Figure 2.10   Greatly simplified process map.

Then, when your team proposes what the process could be in the future with some (or many) additional changes (Figure 2.10) the response from the organization leaders is usually one of great interest.

QUICK WINS

Many short-term improvements, or *quick wins*, can become visible immediately during the process mapping workshop and reviews of the process maps that are generated. The quick win is typically defined as a positive change that can be implemented in a short period of time (two to four weeks), is within the department or team's control, and costs little or nothing to implement. For example, a team that was addressing the problem of sending payment checks for insurance claims to the policyholders was studying the possibility of issuing checks from a remote location instead of the corporate office. Within the first week of the project they had mapped the current process and found several quick wins, including reducing delays caused by inaccurate addresses, printing improvements from a change in the paper stock that was used, and an automated e-mail that was sent to customers when the check was put into the outgoing mail. The bigger improvements from the project were still to come. These few things helped make an impact to customers quickly, and showed the executives that the team was really looking for ways to improve and proving its value to the organization.

Finding and executing a number of quick wins will not be enough to conclude the project and claim that the process has been improved. If all that was needed to improve the process were one or more quick wins, then it is likely that the problem in the charter was not as significant as originally thought.

PROCESS ANALYSIS: ADDING VALUE

A customer will pay money to buy a wrench from a store. She will not pay the store extra money to move that wrench from one shelf to another shelf in the store so it is easier to find during inventory.

The customer will pay the bank to provide a car loan. He will not pay extra money just to get another approval signature from a vice president somewhere in the bank.

These simple examples draw the distinction between process steps that add value and steps that do not. Simply put, value-adding steps in a process are those steps that:

1. The customer will pay for

2. Are done correctly the first time

3. Change the product or output

The customer will not pay you to go back and correct an error before providing the product or service to him. In fact, he will often become annoyed with the delay, and you will lose money in the form of a discounted price, lost repeat business, or lost referrals. The customer will also not pay you for a step in the process that doesn't help transform the output into what she ordered.

Now take your process map and list all the individual steps. Then write next to each whether it is a *value-adding* (VA) step or a *non-value-adding* (NVA) step. Your purpose will be to remove the NVA steps wherever possible. It is also important to list a third category: *value-enabling* (VE) process steps. These are steps that can not be described by the three bullet points above yet are still very important to the organization, that is, without them the opportunity to add value for the customer would be in jeopardy. A prime example of a VE step is regulatory reporting requirements. If you are required by an authority to check some detail in your process before providing your product or service to the customer, this step in the process must be listed as value-enabling and will, of course, not be removed.

This does not mean that anyone can review the process map and just say, "This process step is important to me, therefore it is value-enabling." An honest and objective view must be taken when conducting process analysis. One of the worst and most common answers to the question, "Why do you do it that way?" is "That's the way we've always done it." Such an answer should set the process improvement specialist into motion, uncovering the true needs of the customer, matching the process to them, and looking for gaps. As an example, a company sent every loan application that was over a certain dollar amount to a third party for review and approval. When asked for the reason, the "always done it that way" answer followed. During the study of two years worth of applications, no denials were encountered under a dollar amount much higher than the amount used in practice. The dollar limit was raised to a mutually agreed level, and the company saved over $100,000 a year in fees and postage.

Going back to the example of the second signature on the car loan: if the bank's process is to get that vice president's signature on every loan, the Green Belt in the bank should ask a few questions:

- Is the VP's signature required for a regulatory reason? If so, then we will not be able to eliminate that process; we will have to streamline it. If it is not required for regulatory reasons, why do we require it?

- Is there a waiting period for that VP to sign? Does this wait cause delays in the process? If so, then the VP's signature is a roadblock and needs to be examined further.

- Does the VP sign the approval herself? If she delegates it some or all of the time, then the process could be remapped to route the approval to the designated signer instead of waiting for the VP.

- How often does the VP actually refuse to sign? If the approval is achieved 100 percent of the time, then the staff are doing everything right, and the VP's review may no longer be required.

- What are the circumstances under which the VP does need to take a closer look at the application? If you understand what these are, then maybe the staff could be given permission to process any loans that do not fall into these exception categories.

Just because "we've always done it this way" does not mean that is still the right way to do it!

SPAGHETTI DIAGRAM

Another useful tool to illustrate the current process for the purpose of improving it is the *spaghetti diagram*. This diagram uses a continuous line to trace the path of the process (see Figure 2.11). Watching the flow of the line can be very eye-opening when looking for wasted time, repetition, and redundancy in the work.

The spaghetti diagram is prepared as a view from the ceiling of the room where the work is performed. If work takes place in more than one office or room, the diagram is expanded to include that space. Seeing the process from this point of view is useful in identifying points of overlap or repeated steps within the room(s). There are a number of ways to win in this situation, and most of them are addressed by the eight wastes of lean (see sidebar).

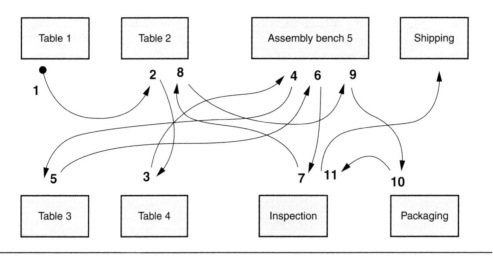

Figure 2.11   Spaghetti diagram of work flow for preparation of one lot of 100 units.

Process mapping is an important foundation for success in any improvement project. Your team's stated objectives may be cost savings, an increase in revenue, shorter delivery time, fewer defects, less rework, or one of many other admirable and useful goals. In reality, the objective of a process improvement project is an improved process that, when adopted fully and followed every time, will produce those quantifiable benefits. The way your process map looks today is not the way it will look ninety days from now.

The Eight Wastes of Lean

1. *Overproduction.* In a factory, this means making more product than is required. Someone has determined the best batch size that will reduce the cost of the raw materials that have to be ordered. The problem is that you tie up money in inventory and take up space with the extra production, and because you have overproduced in one area, you may end up with a shortage in another.

2. *Waiting.* Movement of materials often requires careful scheduling. When some number of products that are going to your customer have to wait for another process to be completed or another part to be combined with them, then you have extended your overall process time and created waste.

3. *Transportation.* Moving parts or people from one place to another to do a different job during the day is a waste of time and motion. The flow of the factory or the office should be tracked using a spaghetti diagram, and improved to reduce transportation.

4. *Overprocessing.* This means doing additional work that does not add value, which increases the cycle time and cost of the process. In a service setting, this includes unnecessary approvals, as described above.

5. *Excess inventory.* Keeping extra inventory in order to account for defects, shortages, spikes in order volume, and unforeseen problems in the process is a direct waste of money.

6. *Motion.* In addition to a poorly designed shop floor, unnecessary motion can also be caused by an untidy workplace. The remedies for this problem are 5S and a visual workplace. The principles of 5S are detailed later in this book, and the transition from 5S to a visual workplace is described in Chapter 7. In short, there is a place for everything, everything is in its place, and the work space is kept clean throughout the day.

7. *Defects.* When defects are created, work has to be done over correctly. This creates a waste of time and energy in correcting the mistake, more time and energy inspecting the rest of the work that was done at the same time, and a waste of the effort that was expended executing the process incorrectly the first time.

8. *Underutilization of human talents.* When a person's skills are not being used in a way that is interesting to him and in a way that he can be productive, there is a gap between today's performance and his potential, and this is a waste.

Team Meeting #1

Plan Half a Day for Team Meeting #1

The first team meeting is intended to unify the team members in pursuit of the project's improvement objectives. It is also intended to be very productive, with two of the project's nine deliverables being produced or, at least, drafted during the half-day session. If a meet-and-greet is needed to acquaint team members with one another, schedule it before meeting #1 takes place. If this is not possible, then spend the first half hour of meeting #1 with one or two of myriad available icebreaker activities. A few good ones are shown in the following table.

Exercise name	How to conduct it	Objectives
Partner introductions	Participants pair up with somebody they did not know or know well before the meeting. Each is asked to learn facts about the other, such as what department they're from, how long they've been with the organization, something they like to do outside work, or some other little-known fact. After a few minutes, each person then introduces the other to the rest of the group and shares these facts.	Meet one new person directly and learn about all others from each other.
Two truths and a lie	Participants write three statements about themselves on paper: two are true and one is not. Facilitator reads everyone's notes, and the other participants guess which statement is the lie.	Learn new facts about similarities in background and experiences, and get the team laughing.
Calliope	Facilitator prepares a list of statements on paper and reads them one at a time to the group. When each item is read, anyone about whom it is true stands and then sits back down. Items could include: has worked here less than one year, has run a marathon, likes Frank Sinatra, likes Bon Jovi, likes Justin Bieber.	Get everyone to stand at least once for the feeling of inclusion. If one item is "has worked here for less than one year," then another should be "has worked here more than one year." Generate some laughter.

It is also recommended that the project sponsor and project leader meet before meeting #1 to make sure the scope of the project is well defined. We stressed the clarity of the project scope in Chapter 1 and have offered the scope contract as a tool to provide that clarity.

During meeting #1, the first order of business is to complete and agree on the contents of the project charter: business case, problem statement, goal statement, scope, project plan, and team roles. Once these are agreed on, the project charter will be shared with the project sponsor, used as a guidepost for the team throughout the project, revised and redistributed as necessary, and enforced when questions arise.

Continued

Continued

We have discussed the importance of the process map, and development of process maps begins in meeting #1. A useful technique is to identify, in any order, all the tasks that must be accomplished to execute the process within the defined scope and to write each step on a sticky note. All these items can then be stuck to a wall in the time sequence in which they are performed. Departmental swim lanes can be added with long pieces of masking tape.

Between meeting #1 and meeting #2, the project leader will assemble the charter and process maps for the team's approval. Meeting #2 follows meeting #1 by one week, so schedule it with everybody now!

Part II

Measure

3

Sufficient Data

A family is getting ready to move to a new city and they are deciding which part of the metropolitan area to choose for their home. They study the area: the distance from the suburbs to downtown, the median home prices for each section of the city, each school's test scores and teacher to student ratio, the number of parks and green spaces and the mileage of paved bike paths, and more. They study these factors in order to estimate how happy and productive they will be in their new home town—that is, in order to make a good decision.

A business owner is deciding how much money to invest in a new service she would like to offer to her clients. She studies competitive data in the target market, the expected amounts of cost and revenue, her current services and whether the new one will make her existing services less attractive, and more. She is studying these variables in order to make the right decision about entering this new phase.

So, how do you know which x and y variables to study? You will sometimes hear, "I know what the problem is, let's just fix it." Well, that person may be correct. Or the assumption could be totally wrong. Or the stated cause may be only one part of the problem. That's why you'll diligently study all the relevant variables in pursuit of the true root cause or causes of your performance problem.

WHERE TO FIND THE x AND y VARIABLES

The variables that you and your team will study are found in the process map. We discussed the SIPOC format for mapping processes in Chapter 2, and the first list of variables is found by using that tool.

Start with the output. The output of your overall process, like those shown in Table 3.1, is a y variable. There may be more than one main output of your process. Further, the outputs of each process step are also y variables. So, now you have your y list. Next, look at the inputs to each step and list those as x variables. The process variables are found inside the flowchart. These are also designated as x because they are parts of the process that produces output.

Once you have listed all your variables, it is time to study them thoroughly by collecting data. Asking the team to study every occurrence of each variable is usually too great a task, especially in a high-volume process. Instead, you will take a sample of the available data.

Math, Variables, and Tomatoes

My basic takeaway from algebra class is that $y = f(x)$: some variable y was produced by a function, or equation, when some other variable x was introduced into that function. By knowing the behavior of the function, I could add an x that I know and predict what y will be. Conversely, if I know what y was produced by the function, then I can determine what x was used.

If $y = 2x + 4$, and $x = 3$, then $y = 2(3) + 4$, or $6 + 4$, so $y = 10$.

So, if $y = 2x + 4$, and we find out at the end of our process that $y = 14$,

then we know $14 = 2x + 4 \rightarrow 14 - 4 = 2x \rightarrow 10 = 2x \rightarrow$ so, $x = 5$.

We can solve the equation forward or backward depending on which variable we know.

Of course, this scenario gets a little trickier when multiple variables are introduced. Growing tomatoes that are big and juicy requires the right amounts of water and sun, the right temperature, the right kind of soil, and a stick to hold the vines. If you change any of these variables, the tomatoes may end up smaller or larger than you expected.

Back to $y = f(x)$. This statement can be extended: if you understand the performance of the process, then you can predict the output given a known input. Yes, it is important to use the right x. It is more important to be sure that the process produces a predictable, reliable, consistent result, that is, that it works the same way every time. If it does not, then even the best x may not produce the desired result. For example, if you have learned that staffing your call center with 85 people produces a call abandon rate of 2.5% on average, and the abandon rate with 95 people is 1.5%, can you be sure that 105 call center representatives will bring you an abandon rate less than 1%? There may be other factors that influence the abandon rate, and 1.5% may be the absolute floor for that metric. Spending money on 10 more phone agents may not bring the desired result and may not be worth the money. The process needs to be studied further.

After you've made sure that the process is in place and is being followed every time, the output of the process may still not achieve the intended target. Why? In order to answer that question, you must study the variables.

SAMPLING

During a project the Green Belt may ask, "How many samples do I need to take?" The purpose of sampling is to gather enough data to draw conclusions about the entire population. For instance, a lawn care company wants to find out how many of its 2.5 million customers have added a dog to the household in the last year so they can decide whether to add carpet cleaning to its service offerings. Asking 2.5 million people could take a long time and might cost a lot of money. Studying a sample of them would help to draw conclusions about the entire population of 2.5 million, saving time and energy.

Table 3.1   Input, process, and output variables from our previous sample processes.

Problem statement	Input variables x_i	Process variables x_p	Output variables y
This is the description of the problem. It is most useful when quantified. A narrative paragraph or bullet points will work.	*These need to be studied to see what impact they have on the output. Only three are shown here for each problem statement; there are likely many more.*	*These also need to be studied for their impact on the output and on the next process step.*	*When the x variables are changed, what impact do those changes have on the output? When you find the best settings, then you have a recipe for success.*
Customer satisfaction with quality of the PKR product was rated 63% last quarter, an all-time low.	• Supplier inputs • Raw materials • Customer orders	• Manufacturing process details • Change orders • Delivery details	• Defect-free product yield • Number and type of defects created • Customer satisfaction score (not a direct output of the process; this is a measure of the voice of the customer)
On-time delivery of D-pipes is 87%: 11% are late and 2% are too early for customers to use.	• Product availability • Delivery process • Vehicles	• Delivery routing process • Delivery schedule • Delays and reasons for delay	• Delivery time (this is best measured in minutes—a continuous variable, not pass/fail) • Customer feedback
Payments made via electronic data interchange cost 1.5 times the budget for accounts in the western United States.	• Accurate transaction prep • Customer-supplied data • Bank-supplied data	• Processing speed or bandwidth • Transaction volume • Timing/schedule of transactions	• Completed transactions • Transaction speed and accuracy • Advance notice of payment

As another example, a flooring company wants to study their process for installation to see if the checklist is being followed. They have 50 installations per day, and can't watch them all. So, they sample the calculated number of installations on random days during the month. This is important because they want to predict the performance of the process every day, not just on the days they are sampling.

- A *population* comprises every possible occurrence: all the people in your organization, every invoice sent to all your customers, every product that comes off your line.

- A *segment* of the population is some subset or category of the larger group: all people in your organization who work in Illinois or who have been with the team less than one year, all invoices that are over $10,000 or that were sent during January, all products that were manufactured in Brazil or that were shipped on time.

- A *sample*, then, is some number of occurrences less than the total population. In order for the sample to enable you to draw conclusions about the population, three factors are needed. The first is that you have a plan to capture a sample that reflects the population and its segments. The second is the sampling strategy. The third factor is the calculated number of samples required. Let's look at each of these elements of the sampling plan.

1. A Random and Representative Sample

A well-crafted sampling plan can have a powerful impact on your study. On the other hand, a plan that is not random or representative can have damaging effects on your customers. For example, if the population being studied has six discernable segments and you sample from only one, then the conclusions you draw from that sample may not reflect the parameters of the full population. The impact of making decisions based on a nonrepresentative sample is that the segments you did not study will not be served and their needs will not be met. To correct this problem you will use *stratified sampling*, wherein samples are taken from each category of the population. Further, you'll use the same proportions that exist in the population for your sample. If, for example, you know that your full population of customers falls into three categories: large (35% of the total), medium (19%), and small (46%), you will want to make sure that a corresponding percentage of your samples comes from those categories.

Next, we want each element of the population to have an equal chance of being chosen for the sample group. This is called a *random sample*, and it is important because there may be more than six categories and we just don't know it yet. For example, if I choose seventeen samples by selecting only the first seventeen from the top of a list, I may only get results that reflect the characteristics of the entries that had some reason for being at the top of the list: those people who arrived first, those people whose names begin with the letter "A," or those items that have the highest prices. Instead, I want to sample all the people or products on the list because I need to know what to expect and, more importantly, my customer needs to know what to expect throughout the entire range of possibilities. In stratified sampling, we'll take a random selection from each category. For your small, medium, and large customers, each of the small customers will have an equal chance of being selected, and you'll still make sure that 46% of all samples taken come from the small customer category.

We plan for a sample that is random and represents the population in order to avoid these and other types of bias. *Bias* occurs when differences are brought into the sampling process that cause unequal representation of the population (see Table 3.2).

Table 3.2 Bias table.

Type of bias	Examples of pitfalls
Selection bias: A strategic issue that needs to be controlled when developing the sampling plan	• Convenience sampling: choosing only the samples that are easy to reach or to obtain • Systematic sampling: choosing samples at the same time each day or from the same point in the process
Environmental bias: Also a strategic issue	• Using data that are no longer relevant because the process has changed or the information is out of date
Non-response bias: Also a strategic issue	• Not reaching all segments • Not everyone responds to surveys
Measurement bias: A tactical issue that needs to be addressed when collecting samples	• Inconsistent definitions and understandings • Rounding off to the nearest number

2. The Sampling Strategy

There are two primary theories of sample collection, and several specific techniques within these two main theories. The main difference between the two theories is the time when the samples are collected.

In *process sampling*, the samples are collected during the process, that is, while the machine is running. For example, defects created during the process that need to be reworked, time required to complete one step of the overall process, waiting time for each person who is on hold, number of orders received each day or each hour within the day, or the number of customers in line at selected intervals throughout the day. The key is that you are collecting data about the process while it is running in order to detect changes, variation, and problems as they are occurring. Knowing when a problem happens is a great first step toward solving that problem.

The appropriate use of process sampling is to track the performance of the process over time. This enables you to spot trends and even make improvements while the process is under way.

In *population sampling*, the samples are chosen at the end of a time period from all the occurrences generated during that period. Examples include the number of applications processed last month, the categories of mistakes made during the past week, history of incomplete or incorrect fields on a loan application, productivity in payments per hour by all members of the team at the end of the month. In population sampling you will often see averages and percentages because the accumulated results are evaluated at the end of the time period, when the process is finished.

The appropriate use of population sampling is to gather statistics about the process for reporting and analysis. The advantages are that you can take your time and study the samples thoroughly at your own speed, and that the reporting of these statistics can be compared to other time periods or to other categories.

Table 3.3 Techniques to ensure random and representative samples.

Sampling technique	When to use	Description
Systematic sampling *(Process)*	With a process that is consistent and shows no evidence of differences or changes in the level of variation during the time period	The frequency for sampling during the process is determined, for example, every fifth occurrence
Rational subgrouping *(Process)*	When you want to uncover differences at specific times or locations in the process	Choosing a group of samples at selected intervals—this enables a study of variation between samples and also within the sample group
Random sampling *(Population)*	When no segmentation factors or categories exist, or none are known when the sampling process begins	Every element of the population has an equal chance of being selected for the sample
Stratified random sampling *(Population)*	When categories exist in the population	A proportional number is chosen for the sample from within each of the population's categories

In order to ensure that you get a random and representative sample, a few techniques are available when developing your sampling plan (see Table 3.3).

3. The Sample Size Calculation

Now, to answer the question that was posed at the beginning of this section: "How many samples do I need?" Remember that the objective of sampling is to collect enough reliable data about a portion of the population to draw good conclusions about the full population. You need to do this so that you can develop your processes to meet the needs of your customers. And you take samples instead of watching and recording every occurrence in the population because you want to achieve these results in ninety days.

The required sample size is based on a few factors:

- The expected amount of variation in the process

- The current defect rate

- The acceptable margin for error

The amount of variation in the process influences the required sample size because a sample taken from a wide distribution, which exhibits a larger amount of variation, may fall farther to the right or left of center than a sample drawn from a process with less variation (see Figure 3.1), and a group of samples has a greater chance of falling on one side of the center in a wider distribution and, as a result, not representing the population accurately (see Figure 3.2).

Figure 3.1   A picture of two processes, one with more variation (left) and one with less.

Figure 3.2   A sample of three points chosen from each distribution.

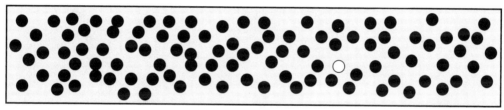

Figure 3.3   Very few defects in sample.

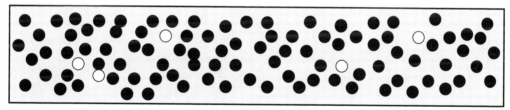

Figure 3.4   A few more defects in sample.

The defect rate of the current process influences the required sample size because it is easier and faster to identify defects in a population when there are very few of them than it is to identify, at a glance, a large proportion of defective products or occurrences. In Figure 3.3, white dots are defects. How easy is it in this example to count the number of white dots in a total of 100? How about in Figure 3.4? How long does it take you to get an exact count of white dots? And in Figure 3.5? Is it getting more difficult? Is it taking you longer to count or estimate? And how about Figure 3.6? How long does it take to get an exact count?

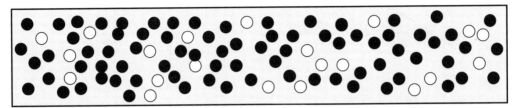

Figure 3.5   Yet more defects in sample.

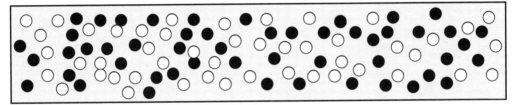

Figure 3.6   Many defects in sample.

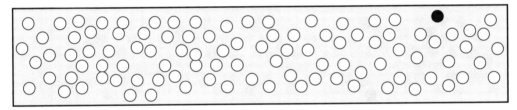

Figure 3.7   All but one defective in sample.

The number of white dots in the preceding four diagrams are 1, 5, 21, and 48, respectively. Did you get them all right? The sample size required to make accurate observations increases as the defect rate increases, just as the time you spent actually counting white dots (sampling!) increased from diagram to diagram.

As an interesting point, the highest sample size requirement is at 50% defective; then the required sample size decreases from 50% to 100% at the same rate that it increased from 0% defective to 50%. Notice the ease with which you are able to determine the number of correct (black) pieces in Figure 3.7.

The acceptable margin for error influences the required sample size because you will need a larger number of samples in order to be more precise in your conclusions. With every element of the population that is not counted, the ability to reflect that population's characteristics exactly is weakened a little. If you want to be 100 percent accurate, that is, no margin for error, you will have to observe every occurrence—the entire population. Reliable conclusions can be drawn about a population through sampling to an acceptable margin for error.

You'll see margin for error expressed in a few ways: plus or minus a percentage (exit polls, marketing studies), plus or minus a number of units (calls received in a day, on-time deliveries), and plus or minus a unit of measure like average or standard deviation

(+/– 4.3 seconds, +/– 1.26 psi). The measure of margin for error determines which of the first two factors listed above (expected variation and current defect rate) you will use in the sample size calculation equation.

If you are using a percentage as your margin for error, you'll use this equation to determine the necessary sample size:

$$n = (2/\Delta)^2 (P)(1 - P)$$

Where:

n = Number of samples required.

2 is used to represent a 95% confidence level (actually 95.5%) so you can say "I am 95% confident in these results."

Δ = The acceptable margin for error, also known as the degree of precision; in this equation it is expressed as a decimal percentage (.03 for 3%).

P = The proportion defective, also expressed as a decimal percentage (.12 for 12% defective).

$1 - P$ = The inverse of the proportion defective (.88 for 12% defective).

If you are using a measure like calls, deliveries, seconds, psi, or something else to describe the variation in the process, you will use this equation:

$$n = (2s/\Delta)^2$$

Where:

n = Number of samples required.

2 is used to represent a 95% confidence level (actually 95.5%) so you can say "I am 95% confident in these results."

s = The standard deviation in the chosen unit of measure; you may have to calculate this if you don't already measure standard deviation for your process.

Δ = The acceptable margin for error, also known as the degree of precision; in this equation it is expressed in terms of the same unit of measure as the standard deviation above.

Table 3.4 shows two sample size calculations, one for a continuous variable—time—and the other for a discrete variable—pass/fail or, in this case, whether the client is still in business or not. Note the difference in the required sample sizes.

Remember that the sample size calculation is only half of the sampling plan. An appropriate sampling strategy that ensures a random and representative sample is equally important in using a sample to draw sound conclusions about the population. When used together, the size and strategy form a sampling plan that will let you see the data more clearly. How easy is it to count defects in Figure 3.8?!

Table 3.4   Examples of sample size calculations using both margin for error formulas. You can see that measuring your process with continuous data means collecting and studying fewer samples!

Calculation of sample size with continuous data	Calculation of sample size with discrete data
A law firm is studying the time required to prepare a specific type of case for trial. The time is measured in hours. The practice group estimates that the amount of variation from one case to the next will be 24 hours (standard deviation), or 3 business days. In order to analyze the process to determine the average time required to prepare for trial without pulling every file in the firm's history, they'll study a sample to draw that conclusion about the entire population.	The same law firm now wants to study their success rate for their clients one year after the trial is handled. They are studying clients who are still in business and those that are not. They have served over 13,000 clients over the years, many of whose companies have changed names. It would be difficult to survey all of them, so they will collect sample data in order to draw conclusions about the population. Historically, one out of four clients for this specific type of trial goes out of business.
Formula: $n = (2s/\Delta)^2$ $n = [(2 \times 24)/8]^2$ *As one business day, 8 hours is the acceptable margin for error* $n = (48/8)^2$ $n = 36$ samples	Formula: $n = (2/\Delta)^2(P)(1 - P)$ $n = (2/.03)^2 (.25)(.75)$ *3 percent margin for error is not uncommon— use 1% if your life depends on accuracy* $n = (66.7)^2 (.1875)$ $n = 833$ samples
Meaning that, after pulling 36 case histories, assuming they are randomly selected and that they represent the process as it is normally conducted, and calculating the average time required to prepare for trial on those 36 cases, they will be able to say with 95% confidence that the next case they handle will require that average length of time in hours to prepare, within plus or minus 8 hours. This can be useful in budgeting administrative support and managing expectations of the client.	Meaning that, after collecting data on 833 of their past clients and learning whether they are still in business or not, they will be able to apply that proportion to the 13,000 clients they've served. If 195 of the 833 have gone out of business, that is a ration of 23.4%. Of their total clients, that would be about 3040 that have gone under, or, more positively stated, about 10,000 who are still in business. This can be a good measure of their success and a good message for marketing as well.

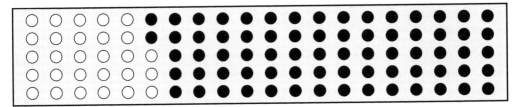

Figure 3.8   The sampling plan brings order to the process.

DATA COLLECTION PLAN

Your goal is to find the root causes of the problem and fix them permanently, and you want to accomplish that in only ninety days. It will be very important to begin collecting data early in the project. It will be very dangerous for our project timeline if you have not collected data on the right variables and have to go back and collect more. On top of that, the people you have asked to collect data will be mighty annoyed if you ask them to start over and do it again. For these reasons, you will develop a detailed data collection plan.

The project team will collect data on three fronts:

- Historical data collection

- Data collection for the project

- Ongoing data collection after the project

A plan is required for each in order to make sure the team is collecting only the data it needs, in the right quantities and units of measure, at the right frequency, and following the established sampling plan.

We have already determined the x_i, x_p, and y variables (input, process, and output) that need to be measured for the process that we are studying. The next step is to gather existing data on those variables from recent history. This will help us to establish a baseline for the performance of your process. If, for instance, you learn through this study that your on-time delivery performance is 85% on Mondays and 96% on Fridays, you already have a clue for process improvement. If you learn that the call center takes an average of 1500 calls a day and that the amount of variation is higher in the early morning and late afternoon than it is around lunchtime, then you have useful information for your staffing model and you have clues for how to improve your overall abandon rate. If you are not already collecting data on the existing processes in your organization, be sure to read Chapter 10 of this book for guidance on setting up useful measures even outside the context of an improvement project.

Historical data collection must be conducted with the same discipline that you'll use in collecting data during the project. Therefore, a data collection plan should be used from the beginning.

THREE PHASES OF DATA COLLECTION

First, you will need to collect historical data about the process in order to understand the magnitude of the problem over time. This also saves time because you will not have to start the project with no data; you have all the history you can find to begin identifying variables that are having an impact on your process output.

The second phase of data collection is the study of variables, which you will conduct during the project. As discussed, it is much better to have too much data than not enough, so your data collection plan for the project may actually include variables that you will not track later because they are not, in the end, proven to have an impact on your process output.

And finally, the team will develop the data collection plan for the ongoing process after the project is complete. If the process is not monitored after project completion, there is a strong risk that the improvements will not be sustained. But at this point, you will only want to track the critical variables—those that are having a proven impact on your process output.

Let's start with history. Somewhere you will be able to find data or information that will help you and the team to establish a baseline for your performance today. In order for you to know how much you have improved at the end of your project, you need to know how you are doing currently. Your customer has expectations, and the frequency with which you are able to meet those expectations determines your level of process capability. Process capability can be expressed in a number of ways: your percent of success, or *yield*, your pass/fail rate, the number of seconds or minutes by which you miss a target, an average score for a team, a measure of variation from that average, the number of defects produced out of one million opportunities, and more. One useful way to express the capability of any process is by using its sigma value. A sigma value can be derived from percentages or defect rates, and you can measure any process with a sigma value. It has another very important strength, however.

For many processes, saying that you are successful 99% of the time is good enough. Letting one inoperative light bulb leave your factory in a box of one hundred may not cause a lot of grief with your customers. Making one billing error on a credit card in eight and a half years (100 months) is probably acceptable. On the other hand, some processes can not allow even one defect out of one hundred, or one thousand, or ten thousand. The process for landing an airplane needs to be a lot better than 99% successful. The same is true in producing pharmaceuticals and medical devices. The strength of the sigma value is that it is robust over 99%; that is, it can be used to measure processes that are already better than 99% successful and it can give you details on how much better the process can still be. In fact, the term *six sigma* refers to a process that is successful 99.99966% of the time. A point to note: when six sigma is translated into a measure of defects, it equals 3.4 defects per million opportunities (DPMO). Tables 3.5 and 3.6 show percentages and defect rates with corresponding sigma values.

Collecting historical data will give you an idea of your process capability today. It will also help you start to identify variables that need to be studied as possible causes of defects and variation. For instance, if you are looking at trend data for a call center, you will see without having to look very closely when your call volume spikes, when your abandon rate is highest, where the most calls are coming from, how many representatives you have on the phones during the day, and much more. These are clues—they are input and process variables that will help you to understand the causes of defects and variation in the process.

Whether or not you have historical data to use, you will need to collect data during the ninety-day project. This data collection could be intense because, as I mentioned, you'll want to collect a large amount of it so that you don't have to go back later and do

Table 3.5   Sigma conversion table for percent yield.

Yield	Sigma	Yield	Sigma	Yield	Sigma	Yield	Sigma
99.99966%	6.0	99.865%	4.5	93.32%	3.0	50%	1.5
99.9995%	5.9	99.814%	4.4	91.92%	2.9	46%	1.4
99.9992%	5.8	99.745%	4.3	90.32%	2.8	43%	1.3
99.999%	5.7	99.654%	4.2	88.5%	2.7	39%	1.2
99.998%	5.6	99.534%	4.1	86.5%	2.6	35%	1.1
99.997%	5.5	99.379%	4.0	84.2%	2.5	31%	1.0
99.996%	5.4	99.181%	3.9	81.6%	2.4	28%	0.9
99.993%	5.3	98.93%	3.8	78.8%	2.3	25%	0.8
99.990%	5.2	98.61%	3.7	75.8%	2.2	22%	0.7
99.985%	5.1	98.22%	3.6	72.6%	2.1	19%	0.6
99.977%	5.0	97.73%	3.5	69.2%	2.0	16%	0.5
99.967%	4.9	97.13%	3.4	65.6%	1.9	14%	0.4
99.952%	4.8	96.41%	3.3	61.8%	1.8	12%	0.3
99.932%	4.7	95.54%	3.2	58%	1.7	10%	0.2
99.904%	4.6	94.52%	3.1	54%	1.6	8%	0.1

Note: Table 3.5 reflects short-term capability. You may have seen a chart with a different conversion—that is the long-term sigma. The difference is an industry standard 1.5 sigma lower for long term than short term because a process will often shift over time. Short-term capability is used for your Six Sigma Green Belt projects.

it again. You'll identify input, process, and output variables through process mapping, and all of these will need to be studied in order to isolate possible causes of defects and variation in your process.

Figure 3.9 shows a sample data collection plan for the project to improve the PKR product's quality performance and customer satisfaction rating.

It is useful to remember a few rules about data collection:

1. Clearly specify *what* is to be collected and *how* it is to be collected. Let the data collectors know what is expected, and tell them *why* this is important.

2. Stick to the plan. After you've developed a good data collection plan, make sure that everyone is following it exactly every time. Variation in the data collection process will make your results unreliable.

3. Keep the data collection forms simple. If you are asking volunteers to help you collect data, this is likely an extra chore for them. Be sure to make it easy for them to help you.

Table 3.6 Sigma conversion table for defect rates.

DPMO	Sigma	DPMO	Sigma	DPMO	Sigma	DPMO	Sigma
3.4	6.0	1,350	4.5	66,800	3.0	500,000	1.5
5	5.9	1,860	4.4	80,800	2.9	540,000	1.4
8	5.8	2,550	4.3	96,800	2.8	570,000	1.3
10	5.7	3,460	4.2	115,000	2.7	610,000	1.2
20	5.6	4,660	4.1	135,000	2.6	650,000	1.1
30	5.5	6,210	4.0	158,000	2.5	690,000	1.0
40	5.4	8,190	3.9	184,000	2.4	720,000	0.9
70	5.3	10,700	3.8	212,000	2.3	750,000	0.8
100	5.2	13,900	3.7	242,000	2.2	780,000	0.7
150	5.1	17,800	3.6	274,000	2.1	810,000	0.6
230	5.0	22,700	3.5	308,000	2.0	840,000	0.5
330	4.9	28,700	3.4	344,000	1.9	860,000	0.4
480	4.8	35,900	3.3	382,000	1.8	880,000	0.3
680	4.7	44,600	3.2	420,000	1.7	900,000	0.2
960	4.6	54,800	3.1	460,000	1.6	920,000	0.1

4. Track the progress of the data collection to make sure it is being conducted properly.

5. Spot-check the data to see if it matches your expectations; just don't start to analyze the data during data collection. You may begin to draw inaccurate conclusions if you start too early. You developed a sampling plan; be sure to stick to it.

6. Use graphs and charts to display the data being collected. Visual images of the data in addition to the tables of information can make it easier for a wide range of audiences to comprehend (see the graph section of Chapter 5).

7. Store or retain all collected data. You may need to analyze it more than once, so don't discard anything during the project.

During the project, you will isolate the critical variables that will need to be controlled throughout the life of the process, even after the project has ended. Using the team's success in identifying and controlling these important variables, you will develop the ongoing data collection plan that the process owners will use on a regular basis. Please see Chapter 9 for details on control and response plans, which will be used to monitor the process that you have just improved.

Performance measure	Operational definition	Data source and location	Sample size	Who will collect the data?	When will data be collected?	How will data be collected?	Other data that should be collected at the same time
Defect rate on PKR	Number of good/number of defective	Inspection line daily	$n = 35$ per day	Tues–Thurs J. Conlan Mon–Wed–Fri T. Buckley	End of shift 5:30 to 6 p.m.	Auditor's checklist and production log	Check paint for runs and pockmarks
Number of defects of type 7	Listed in handbook	Inspection line daily	$n = 50$ per day	D. Ripley	Next day shift startup	Production log	Check type 4
Number of defects of type 4	Listed in handbook	Inspection line daily	$n = 45$ per day	D. Ripley	Next day shift startup	Production log	Check type 7

How will data be used?

Feed defect rate into daily planning and ops briefing

Type 7 and type 4 data shared with project teams

Examples:

- Identification of largest contributors
- Identifying if data is normally distributed
- Identifying sigma level and variation
- Root cause analysis
- Correlation analysis

How will data be displayed?

- I-MR chart for daily defect totals
- u-chart for type 7 and type 4 defects

Examples:

- Pareto chart
- Histogram
- Control chart
- Scatter diagrams

Figure 3.9   Data collection plan.

Data collection is a must for any team that wants to make sustainable improvements based on facts. Armed with the techniques discussed in this chapter, you will be able to produce a useful data collection plan that your team can execute in a timely fashion so you can stay on target to complete your improvement project in ninety days.

4

Consistent Measurement

Thee assembler of an air hose found very few defects during quality control test-ing. Air leaks were detected less than 0.5% of the time. Yet the customer seemed to find many defects. Nearly 18% of all product shipped was found to be leaky. After months of accusations and tampering with manufacturing processes, the cause of the mismatch was finally identified: the customer tested incoming goods using air pres-sure of 5 pounds per square inch (psi) and the manufacturer used only 3 psi. Looking back at the original design, both the customer and manufacturer should have been testing at 3 psi because that is a realistic representation of the load that is put on the device dur-ing its use in the market. Five psi was an extreme number rarely seen in the market that was still in the customer's manual even though the application had changed years earlier. While there are some basic rules of supplier management here that can be discussed and reinforced, this situation is also an example of another problem: the inconsistent meth-ods for measuring a process or product.

PRINCIPLES

Hitting a target is easy if you're standing right in front of it. Move farther away from the target and it becomes more difficult to hit. Make the target smaller and it's even more difficult. If you can hit the target once, that's great. Hitting the target two, three, four, or twenty times is still more difficult. Try standing there all day long and still hitting the target after you're tired and your eyes are weary. Then ask another person to come over and hit the target twenty times; that may be harder or it may be easier for that person than it is for you.

Measuring a process brings some of those same obstacles with it. Here are the main principles that you want to pursue when measuring a process:

- *Accuracy* is the measure of your ability to hit the center of your target.

- *Repeatability* is how well one person hits the target more than once. If you can measure the length of a piece of pipe twice and get exactly the same number, or evaluate the quality of a customer service call the same way if you listen to it more than once, then you demonstrate good repeatability. If, on the other hand, you calculate a different pipe length the second time because you leaned your head to the left instead of the right, or if you score the same call differently the second time because you missed a detail in the conversation, then your repeatability will be low, and it may be difficult for you to make accurate assessments. This makes data collection difficult, and it presents a great challenge when trying to draw sound conclusions using your data. Note that repeatability is not the same as accuracy because even if you do not hit the center of the target every time, your repeatability is still good if you hit the same place as on your previous attempt. The target shown in Figure 4.1 is evidence of a repeatable process, even though the bull's-eye is not being hit.

- *Reproducibility* is how well more than one person can follow the same process with consistent results. I may hit my target in the center every time. If my colleague on the night shift can not hit the same place on the target as I do, then we will have inconsistent results, and our customer will get a different output depending on whether the target was hit during the day or at night. Our goal is meeting the customer's needs every time, not just in the daytime. Even if the two of us are consistent, a third person may hurt the reproducibility score of the process if he or she can not hit the same place on the target that we do.

- *Stability* is your ability to hit the target accurately over a period of time. If you start to weaken late in the day, or if you have surges of accuracy followed by cycles of inaccuracy, then you display a lack of stability in your process.

- *Linearity* is your ability to hit the target throughout the entire range of possible inputs. In the case of target practice, this could mean that you are equally good at hitting a spot in the middle of the target as you are at hitting a spot near the edge. If you picture a tailor's measuring tape made of cloth, that tape may be more difficult to read if thumbprints have smudged the marks near one end, or if the end has been stretched like taffy. A floor scale may not be accurate for weighing vegetables because it is not programmed to be used for weighing anything that weighs less than a person.

Note: Repeatability and reproducibility are often measured together as R&R. *Gage R&R* refers to the repeatability and reproducibility of a measurement system.

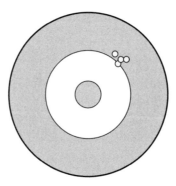

Figure 4.1   Target demonstrating repeatability, but not accuracy.

If the process that you are evaluating, measuring, reviewing, or assessing is difficult to measure for any of the reasons above, it will be important to resolve those issues in order to collect useful data for your project. You will uncover these problems by conducting a *measurement system analysis* (MSA).

MSA METHODS

Stop the project! You have to have reliable data or you risk making bad decisions. If the true amount of variation in your process is not reflected by your measurement, you will not have a true picture of the process and you will not know how bad or good it really is. For example, if your true process variation is 15, and your measurement system adds another 6, you will see overall variation of 21 and conclude that you have even more work to do than you initially thought (Figure 4.2). Thus, you risk tampering with the process in places that are not broken and actually making the process worse!

So, let's find out exactly how well we are measuring the process. I often ask a room full of people, "Exactly what time is it right now, to the second?" The answers are always different. There is only one real, actual time at any given second, yet the measurement systems on our wrists reveal a problem with accuracy all day long. Your MSA will begin with the same question in different words, "Show me how you measure this process."

Take a sample from your workplace. It could be invoices you produce, machined parts, delivery records, a loan application—anything that represents a critical success factor for your organization. Several examples are detailed in the section that follows. You'll need at least ten samples that were created in a similar fashion.

Now gather the people on your team who are responsible for making sure that those items are done correctly. It could be the operator, the inspector, the manager—whoever actually evaluates them before they go to the customer or to the next downstream member of your organization. You should get everybody on that list, if you can. If you can not, you'll need at least three in order to analyze the measurement system.

Next, schedule the operators to evaluate each of the samples once and record their results. It could be pass/fail, evaluation on a continuous scale, a choice from a list of options, or another type of measurement that you do on a regular basis. That is round one. Table 4.1 shows some sample scores for reference.

You can assess accuracy and reproducibility at this point, although you have only one data set, and the possibility that everyone was working extra hard to get it right during the study does often exist. If you can, you should conduct this study with as little fanfare and attention as possible.

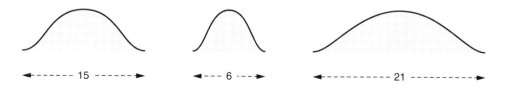

Figure 4.2   Measurement error contributing to perceived variation.

Table 4.1   Sample measurements from MSA study.

Operator	Round 1 scores	Round 2 scores	Round 3 scores
Operator 1	Part 1 151 mm	Part 1 151 mm	Part 1 152 mm
	Part 2 155 mm	Part 2 154 mm	Part 2 155 mm
	. . .	. . .	. . .
	Part 10 152 mm	Part 10 155 mm	Part 10 154 mm
Operator 2	Part 1 152 mm	Part 1 151 mm	Part 1 151 mm
	Part 2 155 mm	Part 2 155 mm	Part 2 155 mm
	. . .	. . .	. . .
	Part 10 154 mm	Part 10 154 mm	Part 10 154 mm
Operator 3	Part 1 150 mm	Part 1 150 mm	Part 1 151 mm
	Part 2 154 mm	Part 2 154 mm	Part 2 153 mm
	. . .	. . .	. . .
	Part 10 154 mm	Part 10 155 mm	Part 10 154 mm

In order to assess repeatability and to get more reliable scores for accuracy and reproducibility, you have to ask the operators to evaluate the same samples again. It is useful to rearrange the samples, let some time pass between rounds, and give the operators fresh score sheets so they will not remember how they assessed each sample the first time.

Next, for the purpose of good statistical analysis, ask them to measure the samples a third time. Once all results are recorded, you can feed them into a statistical software package to calculate the scores for the measurement system, or ask a Six Sigma Black Belt for help if you have one available.

Guidelines for scoring are:

- Total gage R&R should be less than 30% of overall variation in the process. The only real variation that is measured should be that which exists between the individual parts, which is a true picture of variation.

- For repeatability, less than 10% of study variation or, stated another way, a positive calculated score over 90% is desirable, and less than 30% of total study variation is acceptable as long as total R&R does not exceed 30%.

- For reproducibility, like repeatability, less than 10% variation is desirable, and less than 30% is acceptable as long as total R&R does not exceed 30%.

Examples

Project leaders often ask, "How can I possibly conduct a measurement study in my project? I don't have that kind of data." In short, any time two or more people are asked to measure something, there is a chance they will not do it the same way. And it's also useful in my reply to replace the word "measure" with "evaluate," "assess," or "review." This makes the process of measurement seem less about quantification of variables and more relevant to many processes. Here are a few examples:

Dripping paint on car doors. A team of quality checkers was asked to evaluate the paint job on a number of car doors. There were ten doors, all were white, and all were on the driver's side. Each operator scored the doors pass or fail and selected reasons for failure. Then they were asked to leave the room, and the doors were shuffled in order where they were standing against the wall. The second and third times the operators scored the doors, they didn't always agree with their previous assessments (repeatability problem), nor did they all evaluate some of the doors the same way (reproducibility problem). The quality control manager had provided a master score of pass or fail for each of the doors tested, and the operators did not always match that score either (accuracy problem). If an operator incorrectly approves a door, the customer can be unhappy and complain. If an operator incorrectly fails a door, unnecessary rework will be done, and the assembly process, as well as the delivery of that vehicle, may be delayed. The next step was to develop very clear guidelines on what is and is not acceptable for the various failure modes and calibrate the operators in their evaluations.

Newspaper delivery. A trucking company agreed with its customer, a major metropolitan newspaper, to a specific, measurable objective. Every truckload of newspapers had to be dispatched and moving within six minutes after the last bundle of papers was wrapped on the loading dock. When the manager and the customer measured a sample of the process every month, only 85% of truckloads were meeting the six-minute requirement—not a good performance, and one that was going to cost the trucking company a portion of its incentive. A Six Sigma Green Belt studied the process and found that over 97% percent of all truckloads were dispatched and moving within seven minutes, so the additional 12% was just missing the customer's requirement by one minute. It occurred to the Green Belt that a minute comprises sixty seconds and, unless those seconds are measured at the beginning of the time period and at the end, the overall time can be miscalculated. The method of measuring the time was a digital clock on the wall in the dock area. The time was shown as 00:00, hours and minutes only. The team agreed to install a new clock, one that also displayed seconds (00:00:00). After one week, the trucking company's performance against the six-minute dispatch requirement improved from 85% to 98%, *without changing the process at all.* Clearly, the clock on the wall was causing the measurement error and nearly cost the trucking company money in penalties.

Plastic molding. A defect often found in a plastic injection molding process is *splay,* where the plastic does not harden uniformly and waves are visible in the finished product. Customers will reject a product that shows splay because the integrity of the plastic is questionable. One manufacturer of one-inch square plastic pieces found, through its quality control processes, two thirty-gallon trash bags of product that was defective due to splay in one two-week period—money down the drain. Upon further inspection by the department manager, however, much of that product was found to be not, in fact, defective according to the agreement the company had with its customer. The products had been evaluated too strictly. The manager checked the process for inspection with all seven operators using three sample batches of parts. Each batch was evaluated three times by each operator and the repeatability scores were good. However, reproducibility was very low, indicating that some operators had a different standard for approval than others. The manager brought the operators into a meeting to review the customer's specification, and went further, creating a visual aid with examples of passable product and product that is not acceptable. After another two-week study, the amount of defective product due to splay was able to fit neatly into a sandwich bag.

HR exit interviews. A call center had a large amount of employee attrition. Sometimes the metric showed that as many as 60% of people hired within the last six months would leave the company. In order to remedy this problem, the managers agreed to study the causes of the attrition through the process of exit interviews, asking questions like "Why are you leaving?" After several months, the list of reasons for leaving was long and, when charted, showed no specific reason as significantly larger than any other. The length of the list of reasons was troubling to the director, who asked the HR team why there were so many categories. The team indicated that they had brainstormed those categories and started the study with all of them in order to see which ones turned out to occur most frequently. As the director traveled from site to site, HR team members were observed conducting exit interviews, and often the departing employee's comments would be interpreted differently by the director and the interviewer. If one person said, "I'm leaving because I got another job offer from a friend across town," the interviewer could record that as *better pay, better opportunity, distance to work, family/friend referral,* or *geographic preference,* all of which were categories available for selection. The director and the HR team reviewed the data collected from the time the exit interview process began and decided on a much smaller list of primary categories that were easily distinguishable for categorization. Additional details were then recorded within those categories. As a result, the team was able to pinpoint the biggest reasons for employee departure and target them for improvement.

Truck hood gaps. In manufacturing a highway truck, there are allowable tolerances around the truck's hood where it meets the cab of the truck. Too big a gap will allow contaminants into the engine compartment, and too small a gap will prevent the hood from opening. A Six Sigma Green Belt took the assignment of measuring the truck hoods on the completed line at the end of every day. A six-foot-tall man (1 meter, 83 cm), he measured the hood gaps with a wooden ruler at eye level on both sides of the truck. As a diligent Green Belt, he then went back through the entire lot with a new page of paper and recorded those measurements again. Alas, he found his repeatability to be in the low 70s. What could be done? A metal ruler with laser etchings improved his repeatability to 93%. Now, in order to be sure that this process could be continued capably after he had moved on to his next project, he asked another operator to measure the truck hoods. Using the laser-etched metal ruler, she had a respectable repeatability score of 87%. The reproducibility score between the two was not great, though—only 81%. The Green Belt wondered if the difference might have something to do with her stature at five-foot-two (1 meter, 57 cm). Having to look up at a ruler that she was holding over her head might have led to the mismatch. What could be done? A set of dial calipers was employed.

Rolling the calipers out to touch the sides of the hood and cab of the truck and then bringing the dial down to eye level gave their reproducibility score a boost into the mid 90s. Their individual repeatability scores also improved with this new method, which did not depend as much on vision as the rulers. The next solution was a set of calipers with a digital readout, making mistakes practically impossible.

FIXING THE ERRORS

As described in the examples above, action must be taken to make the measurement system more accurate before continuing with the project. You can correct the problems that you find by actually running a project within the project: *define* the scope of the problem and its current status, *measure* the amount of variation through a gage R&R study, *analyze* the causes of the measurement system errors and variation, *improve* the measurement system with solutions to each of these problems and a test of the improvements, and *control* the new process through updated work instructions and ongoing measurement.

You may even want to study the measurement systems all around your organization outside the context of an improvement project. That is a good idea, and it can be very helpful in finding more opportunities for improvement projects.

Team Meeting #2

Plan a Full Day for Team Meeting #2

The second team meeting takes place only one week after the first, so everything should still be fresh in the minds of the team members. It is likely that you will need a full day for meeting #2.

The project leader will bring the updated charter to the meeting for the team to review and approve. You can change the project charter if needed. If changes are necessary, preserve the original and make the modifications on a new copy with approval of the project sponsor.

A thorough review of the process map takes place during meeting #2, and analysis for value-adding and non-value-adding steps will be very useful at this time. It is likely that one or more quick wins can be uncovered during the second team meeting. These should be listed, tested, implemented, and celebrated. Your team is gaining momentum!

The team must devise the data collection plan for historical data that will be gathered and for data collection that will take place during the project. A list of the variables that will be studied can be generated during process mapping, so meeting #2 is an excellent time to match these two steps together.

At least one opportunity for measurement system analysis will be revealed when preparing the data collection plan. Script it according to Chapter 4 and schedule it to be conducted as soon as possible. You have a ninety-day time frame for this project, and every day is important.

Data collection begins immediately following meeting #2 and any MSAs that have to be conducted, and the team will continue to collect data throughout the project.

Between meeting #2 and meeting #3, the project leader will calculate the appropriate sample sizes for data collection using the formulas presented in this book. Meeting #3 follows meeting #2 by four to six weeks depending on the time that is needed to collect the required sample.

Part III

Analyze

5

List of Possible Causes

Good improvement projects that I have seen and led have been successful in part because the teams have taken the time to list possible causes of defects and variation rather than making a decision based on incomplete facts, insufficient data, anecdotal evidence, historical information, one customer's complaint, the boss's assertion, or someone's gut feeling. Making the effort to acknowledge possible causes of the problem that don't fall into these categories enables the team to expand its point of view in search of solutions. It is sometimes true that a gut feeling turns out to be correct. It is also very important to prove that the identified causes are really the *true* causes before making changes to the process.

A very useful tool in listing possible causes is the channeled brainstorming exercise known as the *fishbone diagram*, or Ishikawa cause-and-effect chart. Pictured in Figure 5.1, this visual aid used in this exercise bears a resemblance to a fish skeleton, and it is used to collect information in categories.

If I were to ask a group of people, "What is wrong with the local dining facility?" I would get a wide range of answers concerning the quality of food, availability of seating, prices, hours of operation, cleanliness, customer service, and more. It would then be

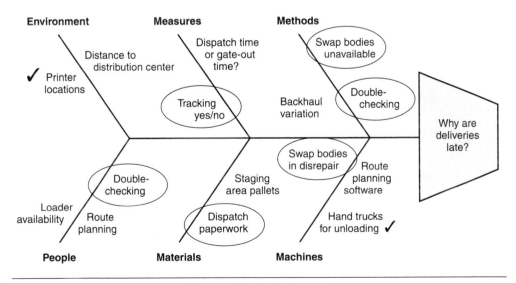

Figure 5.1 Fishbone diagram for late deliveries.

my job to collate and analyze these pieces of information, and it might take me a long time to do it. The fishbone process makes it possible to gather all this information in a timely, accurate, and categorized manner with the help of the team members, who can be engaged throughout the meeting.

The fishbone process is best conducted in a team meeting (meeting #3 in this book, or a separate meeting that takes place between meetings #2 and #3), though it has been done asynchronously at times through an exchange of e-mails. With everyone in the room, the meeting facilitator draws the diagram on a wall or projector and writes the specific problem in the "head" of the fish. The specific problem may be the problem statement from the project charter, or it may reflect one element of the process that needs further investigation. And the head of the fish should always show a question, so we know that we are looking for answers to why the problem is happening. Examples could be:

"Why do we have a 6% abandon rate in our call center?"

"How are our customers able to miss the instructions that we print on our product?"

"Why are deliveries late?"

"What causes the main complaint that we get about our service?"

Very specific problem statements are better because they sharpen the focus of the group and because they usually take less time to complete than a general problem statement. It is almost always better to divide a large problem into separate fishbone discussions and tackle the separate elements of the problem in pursuit of the overall objective than to try and boil the entire ocean at once. In fact, the example in Figure 5.1 about late deliveries might even prove to be too broad depending on how many types of deliveries there are at your organization. This is a very important reason for studying the variables in the process from the beginning of the project, starting with historical data collection.

Now the discussion will focus on one area at a time. Each main line coming off the fish's central backbone will serve as a major category of defects or causes to our problem. Using six bones, as Figure 5.1 does, originates from a set of agreed on, generic categories that represent nearly all categories of defects:

- Materials

- Environment

- Measures

- Methods

- Machines

- People

Your purpose is to find the variables that might be causing problems in your process, so you use these categories to group the possible causes and help you focus on differences, variation, and the impact that the specific elements of the process are having on the output. The question you will want to ask the group over and over during this meeting is, "What is it about our [category] that has an impact on our [problem]?"

Materials might include the raw materials and packaging in a factory, the information supplied to a call center representative, or anything else that is used or consumed in the process. "What is it about the *materials* we use that has an impact on our *complaints*?"

Environment can mean the geographic distance between offices and customers, the amount of cold or noise in a work area, or anything else that impacts the process due to working conditions. "What is it about our working *environment* that has an impact on our *abandon rate*?"

Measures are important because the way one department measures its success can have an impact on that department's behavior that causes negative results in another area. For example, on-time shipments can be increased by increasing the amount of money paid to freight expediters. So, while the shipping department score rises, the finance score falls. "What is it about our *measures* that has an impact on our *material cost variance*?"

Methods leads us to analyze the established procedures in our workplace. There may be things we've been doing for years that are actually causing problems. "What is it about our *methods* that has an impact on our *lost time injuries*?"

The *machines* category really refers to anything electrical or mechanical that is used in the process. "What is it about our *machines* that has an impact on our *defect rate*?"

I saved the *people* category for last because, while it is possible that the problems in the process are caused by the people who are performing it, it is often more likely that the methods, machines, environment, measures, and materials that have been provided by the organization's leaders to those who are performing the process have caused those people to make an error. W. Edwards Deming made his famous point that the vast majority of mistakes made in the workplace are failures of systems and processes, not the people. It is, therefore, in the best interest of the organization to build processes that work all the time and that eliminate the opportunity to perform the process incorrectly. "What is it about our *people* that has an impact on our *product returns*?"

You do not have to use these generic categories for your discussion. If your team is resolving a problem with the rate of defects created, and you feel it would be better for you to use categories in your discussion like *maintenance*, *packaging*, *information technology*, and *shift changes* to focus your discussion, you are free to customize the diagram. Just picture yourself asking the team, "What is it about our *shift changes* that impacts our *defect rate*?" and "What is it about our *information technology* that impacts our *defect rate*?"

FISHBONE CHARTING
IS NOT THE END OF THE PROCESS

Once the team has added information to the "bones" of the fishbone chart, take some more time to identify key variables that need to be studied further. There are several clues to finding these items:

- Look for items that appear more than once on the chart.

- Look for items you had not thought of before and that have piqued the interest of the team during the meeting.

- Use your experience and intuition to highlight items that are likely to have an impact.

- Don't discard anything as irrelevant unless you have proof supported by data that there is no link between the possible cause listed and the problem being addressed.

This is not the end of the process. Root causes are not proven through brainstorming. You will have to analyze the data that are being collected by your team and test the validity of the possible root causes. Chapter 6 will detail the methods for root cause verification.

The fishbone exercise can be useful in identifying more quick wins for your project. If something is identified during this meeting that requires immediate action, that is within the control of the team, and that, when tested, does not cause any unintended consequences in another area of the organization, execute that change and report your success!

WHY–BECAUSE TOOL

Another simple way to look at the problem and possible causes is the *why–because graph*.

As with the fishbone diagram, start by asking, "Why does this problem happen?" You may get one answer, or two, or more. Show all those answers on the chart. Then, one by one, ask the same question for each: "Why does *this* happen?" Continue the process until you get to something actionable or something for which you don't know the answer. This is another great way to identify possible root causes for further study and validation. The example shown in Figure 5.2 would continue by asking four more questions like:

"Why did we decide that keeping each step brief is a good idea?"

"Why do the customers have to organize their responses into our five categories?"

"Why do we ask the sorting questions first?"

"Why do we wait to ask the personal questions?"

The questioning would continue until something can be changed for the better. A frequently used rule of thumb is to ask *why?* at least five times. This is known as the *5 whys* approach, and is used to dig deeper and deeper into the problem until you find something that can and should be changed for the better.

Conducting a Fishbone Discussion

Over the years, I have found that successful Six Sigma projects are those that include a good fishbone discussion. Getting the right group of people together to discuss the possible causes of the problems in the process really helps to move the team toward successful resolution of these issues and toward project completion in a reasonable amount of time—ninety days. Steps for conducting a good fishbone session are:

1. Give everybody advance notice for the session, including instructions and desired outcomes. "On Tuesday at 9:00 we will meet in training room 1 for ninety minutes. The purpose of this meeting is to uncover possible root causes for our late deliveries problem. Please bring notes about what you think may be causing delays, and we will go through them in a systematic way using the fishbone diagram. After listing and discussing the causes, we will test them over the next several days to determine which of them really has the greatest impact on late deliveries, and this will help us solve the problem."

2. Decide whether you will use the six general categories on the fishbone (materials, methods, machines, metrics, environment, people). It may be more appropriate to use categories that are more specific to your process, like hours of operation, customer service, returns process, dock layout, IT support, or any others that are suitable for your purpose.

3. Begin the meeting by describing the fishbone diagram. Draw the diagram on a whiteboard, chalkboard, or a few easel pad pages taped to the wall (you'll need more space than one flip chart), or broadcast the page you are creating on a computer through a projector onto the wall or screen. You'll have to type pretty fast, though, and make sure the words are large enough to be seen at the back of the room. Using a computer is also helpful if you have people on a conference call for this meeting.

4. Write the problem in the form of a question in the head of the fish so no one loses sight of what you are discussing during the meeting: "Why do we have late deliveries?"

5. There are two approaches to filling in the chart. The first is to capture each item that the participants give you on the fishbone diagram in the category that fits that item best. The second is to go through the diagram bone by bone and ask the group for items that fit into each category. I prefer the first method because there is less of a chance that something listed and brought to the meeting by any individual will not be shared with the room. It is important that the team does not get hung up on which bone to write each item in. In fact, if a specific problem fits into more than one category, or bone, write it in both places; it could be an indication of its importance.

Continued

Continued

6. Circle items that appear more than once. And, through discussion, determine which items are likely to have a great impact on the process, and circle them as well. This does not mean they are the only variables that will be tested, though they are good variables with which to begin the analysis.

7. Thank the team and begin testing with their help.

The fishbone session can be included in project team meeting #3, the description of which follows this chapter. It can also be done outside the context of an improvement project any time that you want to combine the brainpower of your team, your peers, your stakeholders, your customers, or your adjacent process owners to look for a solution to a specific problem.

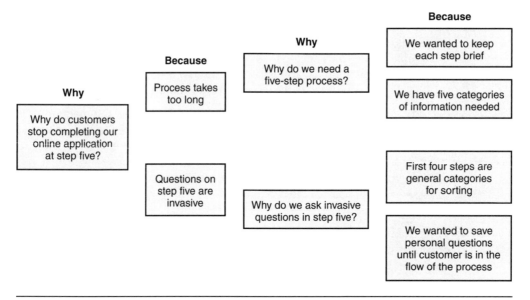

Figure 5.2   Example why–because graph.

By continuing to ask *why?* in Figure 5.2, the organization may find that they only need two screens, or even one, for the customers to complete, or they may find that asking the personal questions earlier in the process works better for their customers. One of the best answers to get in a why–because chart is, "We've always done it that way." This is a great opportunity for change because today's process and today's customer will almost definitely be different than those that were in place when the old version of this process was started.

GRAPHING DATA

While you are collecting data on your process, it is useful to represent the data on a visual chart. Seeing the data charted will often give you great clues concerning causes of variation and defects. Graphs are really essential to data analysis for a number of reasons. By visually displaying your data, they make it more understandable to the human mind. Graphs can take complex data and structure it into easily interpreted pictures. There are a variety of graphs to choose from based on the type of data that you have and the output you are looking for. Here are some commonly used graphs.

Time Series Plot

Many of the charts that we commonly see in use today can be classified as time series plots. *Time series plots* show the progression of data or a process over time (see Figure 5.3). They are extremely easy to build and to comprehend. For your own data analysis, a time series plot can help you understand a great deal about your data or process. Not only can these charts show you variation, they can also identify useful indicators such as long- or short-term trends and seasonality.

Scatter Plot

Many times, the number of occurrences can say a lot about your data. Suppose you want to know how many times something occurred within your data set at a specific level. *Scatter plot* charts are an excellent visual aid for viewing all your data together at one time. Variables are assigned along the *x* axis (horizontal) and *y* axis (vertical), while points within the chart are represented by a designated symbol. Each symbol indicates

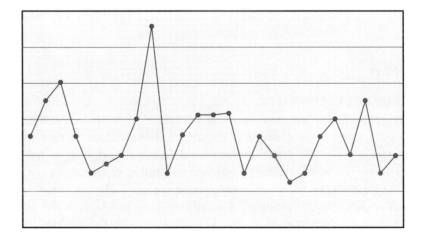

Figure 5.3   Time series plot example.

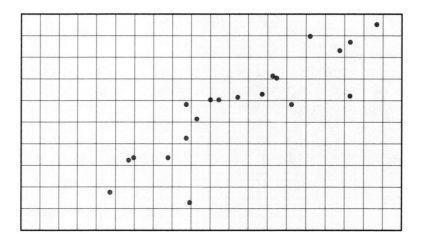

Figure 5.4   Scatter plot example.

one occurrence of an *x–y* pair. Observing where and how many times something takes place can help you pinpoint problem areas or areas deserving further analysis. In the example in Figure 5.4, the number of people in the store at various points during the day is plotted on the *x* axis across the bottom, and the number of sandwiches bought is plotted on the *y* axis from bottom to top. It appears from the chart that the number of sandwiches bought increases as the number of people in the store increases. Note that this is not a time series plot. The points plotted in this graph could have occurred at any time during the period of data collection; they are not intended to show time sequence from left to right. Note also: it is very important not to conclude definite causal relationships between predictor variables on the *x* axis and response variables on the *y* axis when using scatter plots. These graphs should be used as an exploration tool when viewing your data, not as a tool that shows cause and effect.

Pareto Chart

A *Pareto chart* may look at first like a simple bar chart. When it is used properly, it can provide a large amount of information about your data. They are best utilized for categorizing defects. Look at the example in Figure 5.5. The chart shows reasons for defective paint on a car door. The graph displays the defects left to right from most common to least common. The *y*-axis on the left shows the number of defects by count, and the *y*-axis on the right shows what percentage those defects make up among all defects. The cumulative percentage line is also inserted into the graph to show the percent of all defects as each new defect category is added from left to right. By graphically displaying your data from most common to least common, Pareto charts give you the opportunity to focus attention on your most vital defects. Frequency of defects is only one way that

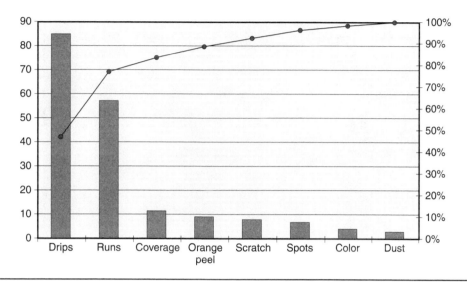

Figure 5.5   Pareto chart example for automotive paint defects.

the Pareto chart can be sorted. It can also be created to show the most severe defects, those requiring the most time to repair, or the most costly. For identifying and quantifying the sources of a problem, the Pareto chart is usable in and outside the context of an improvement project.

Main Effects Plot

We are often asked to compare data from different groups. A good tool for showing this segmented analysis and how the process performs under different conditions is the *main effects plot*. The data are sorted into categories that are displayed on the x-axis, and the data in each category are evaluated separately. The mean of the data for each category is shown by the dots on the connected line, and the overall mean of the full data set is shown as a dashed line. This graph can provide a good snapshot of a process to identify significant differences in performance among groups. The example in Figure 5.6 shows the number of orders that are canceled at a distribution center in Brazil, and the cancellations are sorted by the day of the week. You can see that cancellations are more common on Saturday, and the next step in improving your process might be to answer the question—what is special about Saturday? Note: days are listed in alphabetical order.

Interval Plot

An interval plot can be used to show your data in greater detail than the main effects plot. The *interval plot* shows the mean of the data set in each category and the confidence

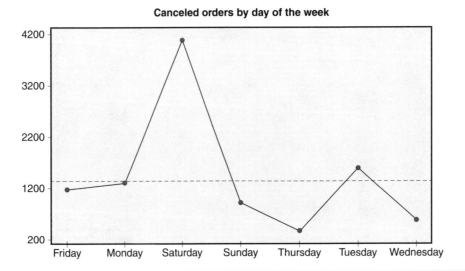

Figure 5.6   Main effects plot example.

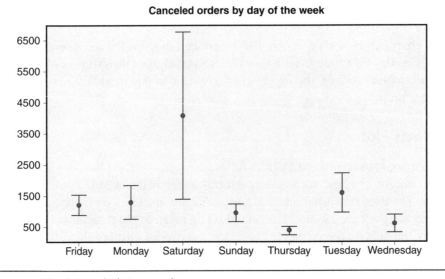

Figure 5.7   Interval plot example.

interval for the mean or the standard error for the data set. This can help to identify the greatest and smallest amount of variation among the categories. The example in Figure 5.7 is from the same data set from the distribution center in Brazil. Now, not only can we see that the average number of canceled orders is greater on Saturday, but also that the number of cancellations on a given Saturday can reach a number much higher than that average. We can also see that the number of canceled orders seems very predictable on Thursday. If we compare Thursday to Saturday, we may find a way to improve the process.

Box Plot

Sometimes called the *box and whisker plot*, this graph represents the structure of the data distribution (see Figure 5.8). The median of the data set is shown by the bold line between the two sections of the box. This means that 50% of the data points lie on the left side of that line and the other 50% are on the right. The data points that are between 0 and 25% of all the data points are in the left-hand whisker, and the data points that lie between 75% and 100% of the data points are in the right-hand whisker. The lowest value in the distribution will be the leftmost point of the left-hand whisker. The highest value in the distribution will be at the end of the right-hand whisker. If there is an extremely low or high value that is mathematically calculated as an outlier, it will be shown as a star. The solid dot near the middle of the distribution represents the mean, or average, of the data points. In a normal distribution, the mean will almost always be the same as the median, so this dot will be close to the bold line. Normally distributed data will also show boxes of uniform size and whiskers of similar length. Showing a box plot to a roomful of people is often risky because you may spend as much time explaining how to read the graph as you will explaining the data.

Multi-Vari Charts

Multi-vari charts show variation within sample data sets and between sample data sets and are, thus, very powerful screening tools for variables in pursuit of possible root causes (see Figure 5.9). There are several ways to graph the data, and almost all of them

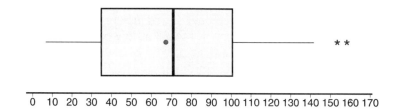

Figure 5.8   Box plot example.

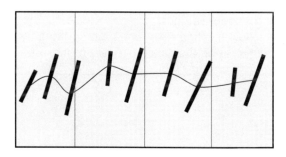

Figure 5.9   Multi-vari chart example.

show a vertical or slanted line bisecting a curve at spedified intervals—the center of each line is the mean of the data set—and the length of the line indicates the amount of variation (usually standard deviation) for the data. Longer lines illustrate more variation within the data set. You are able to compare the centers of the data sets shown to see which is closest to desirable and which are similar to each other. You are also able to compare variation to see which data set is more predictable. A predictable process that is not centered is preferred to a process that has the right average and a high amount of variation. This is because the predictable process, if untampered with, can be repositioned to the target. Multi-vari charts are used to identify positional, temporal, and cyclical variation. *Positional variation* is a change in performance based on the location of the process. *Temporal variation* is a change in the process over time. *Cyclical variation* is a change in the process with a repeating pattern. Studying all of these sources of variation will give the team clues for finding the root causes of the problem.

Team Meeting #3

Plan Half a Day for Team Meeting #3

After collecting the necessary sample, calculated in Chapter 3, the team needs to meet for the purpose of analyzing the data. The third team meeting will follow the second by up to six weeks depending on the time required to collect sufficient data. It is a very good idea to send materials to the team prior to the meeting so that you don't have to spend too much time getting everybody back up to speed during the meeting.

The main purpose of meeting #3 is to identify the possible causes of variation, defects, delays, and other problems that you have stated in your project charter. The team will use the data that you have collected, as well as any other facts that have been gathered during the project, to make a list of all possible causes, not just the ones that someone believes to be responsible for the problems. If a separate meeting has taken place for the fishbone discussion, use the results of that exercise for this discussion. If the fishbone diagram has not yet been completed, you may use this time for that exercise.

If the team has identified any quick wins, remember to test them, make those positive changes, and document them. If the project charter needs to be updated because the scope has been refined, make the necessary revisions in a new version of the charter, preserving all prior versions.

Meeting #4 will follow meeting #3 by one month, giving the project leader time to conduct statistical analysis on the data to validate root causes.

6

Verified Root Causes

Everything your project team has been doing up to this point has prepared you to isolate the root cause or causes of the problem you are experiencing in your process. This is a very exciting time, knowing that you are about to find, prove, and resolve these issues—and all within ninety days!

What would you give to be able to predict the output of your process? How valuable would it be for you to tell your customer exactly what to expect and then be able to deliver it every time? What if you could see which team, which machine, which location, which tool, or which day was giving you the most trouble and then fix it fast? This is the strength of root cause validation—enabling you to control your process.

First let's look at what you've done. You formed a team of motivated people and subject matter experts to help you. Then you recorded your assessment of the problem and your expectations for improvement in the project charter. You mapped your current process so that everyone could have the same picture of the work as it is done today. You identified the variables in the inputs, process steps, and outputs, and started to measure them in detail. So, you have data—facts that you can use to make informed decisions. Now it is time to analyze that data.

A note on the fishbone discussion from Chapter 4: It is a very useful exercise in identifying possible root causes. The items found through the fishbone process need to be validated in order to be proven as the real root causes. If you do not validate them through statistical analysis, you risk tampering with variables that are really not causing the problem, and you risk missing the opportunity to fix variables that really are. In other words, the project will fail.

BUSINESS PROBLEM INTO STATISTICAL PROBLEM

When you look at the problem statements we listed in Chapter 1, they are very familiar and easy to explain. They are also written in easy-to-understand English sentences. These are business problems, and they require business solutions. If it were easy enough to answer the business problem with a business solution, there would be no need for the Six Sigma project. You decided that a project was necessary because the process is in place, it is understood by all members of the team, it is being followed every time, it is not producing the desired results, and you don't know why. So, you will need to restate the problem without a view of the business at all in order to find the right solutions.

Table 6.1   Key to abbreviations for variables in canceled order problem.

Day of the week	Monday = M	Tuesday = T	Wednesday = W	Thursday = R	Friday = F
Business region	Northeast = 1	Southeast = 2	Midwest = 3	Northwest = 4	Southwest = 5
Customer type	Distributor = D	End user = E			
Product	JKG	RTP	SQC	HIW	
Season	Winter = Wt	Spring = Sp	Summer = Su	Fall = Fl	

For example, suppose your problem statement is: the number of canceled orders this year exceeds the budgeted amount by 40% (the budget for cancellations is 9% of all orders). There is no problem understanding this the way it is written. So you've identified variables and started collecting data. You found that canceled order rates are highest on Fridays, highest in the southwest region, and highest for product JKG. Further, you found that canceled order rates are lower from distributors versus end users, lower in the summer than other seasons, and lowest on Mondays. This is very useful information—information you did not have prior to developing and following your data collection plan.

Let's name these variables. First of all, we'll call the *canceled order rate* CO, calculated as the percent of total orders that end up being canceled.

There's one other factor that we found to be interesting during the data collection. The cancellation of orders seems to be higher when the price of the product is higher. Prices (¶) will change based on order volume, distributor business versus direct customer purchases, credit terms, and more. So there is variation in the pricing, and we've found that higher prices seem to bring a greater level of cancellations.

When you look at this problem now, with our translated variables, it may look something like this: CO is high for F, 2, JKG, and higher ¶; CO is low for M, D, and Su (see Table 6.1 for abbreviations).

Why is it useful to look at the problem in this way? Putting on statistical blinders will enable the team to keep its focus on the variables that have been identified during the project and not on any other issues like the personalities involved. You are not looking for excuses; you are looking for causes.

STATISTICAL HYPOTHESIS TESTING

If you ask your customers, "What is most important to you?" you might hear several responses. Some may say product safety, some may say features, some may say timely delivery. What the customer says might not always be exactly accurate, though. When you look instead at their buying behavior, you might see that price is most important, or you might pick up on a trend based on a current marketing buzz. There is danger in taking the customer's statement and acting on it without proving it through analysis first.

The same is true with process improvement. A problem might seem to have an easy fix once you've mapped it. It is important to verify that through data analysis, though, so you do not fix the wrong thing or leave the real cause unfixed.

Now that you have your data and have translated the problem into a statistical one (CO is high when . . .) you will test your variables to see which are really causing the defects and variation in the process. There are many statistical tests that can be performed on a set of data depending on the types of data that you are analyzing. We will focus on four specific tests that are used most often (see Table 6.2).

Let's look at our canceled orders problem. Our output variable is canceled order rates, CO. This is a continuous variable because it is measured on a continuous scale (15.23% of total, 11.6% of total, and so on); it is not measured by counting or categorizing. If we were measuring the number of canceled orders, this would not be a continuous measure because you can only cancel whole orders (one, two, three, and so on).

Now we want to find out the reasons why orders are canceled, so we study the variables. Our input variables are *day of the week*, *geographic region*, *product*, *customer type*, and *season*. None of these is continuous. There are seven days in a week, usually only five business days, and the order will be canceled on one of those days, not in between. There are five regions in our model. There are two customer types, and there are four seasons. These are counted or categorized inputs, known by Six Sigma practitioners as *discrete measures.*

There is one continuous input variable—the price. Price, in dollars, is continuous because it is a measure that can be subdivided and still have meaning. Other useful continuous measures for other business problems are shown in Table 6.3.

Our variables need to be tested to see which of them is (or are) really causing a problem. Let's begin right away—you only have ninety days!

First, the day of the week. We'll use ANOVA, short for *analysis of variance*, to study this because it has a continuous output—canceled order rate—and categorized inputs. In

Table 6.2   Four common statistical tests for data.

Name of test	Purpose	Types of data	Example
Regression analysis	"The Predictor" shows what you can expect	Used for a continuous input and a continuous output	Does the amount of revenue increase as your marketing spending increases?
Two-sample T-test	"The Boxer" shows who is better	Used for a continuous output produced by two operators	Which shift—day or night—produces more defective products?
ANOVA	"The Sorter" shows which category is best	Used for a continuous output produced by multiple operators or categories	Which type of loan—car, home, small business, or equity—presents the greatest default risk?
Chi-squared	"The Scales" show expected values versus actual	Counted units divided into categories	In which geographic region do we lose the most accounts?

Table 6.3   Continuous and discrete measures for business problems.

Continuous variables	Discrete variables
Time required to complete a task	Number of customer service representatives working during a specific hour of the day
Money spent on advertising	Categories of loan applications: large, medium, small
Pounds per square inch, miles per gallon, applications processed per employee, or other such productivity measures	Number of invoices processed during a week, number of complaints received, number of errors made, or other *counted* results of the process

```
                      Individual 95% CIs For Mean
   Level       Mean   +---------+---------+---------+---------
   1-Monday    0.08503 (---*---)
   2-Tuesday   0.12446                (----*---)
   3-Wednesday 0.12730               (---*---)
   4-Thursday  0.14495                    (---*---)
   5-Friday    0.14404                   (----*---)
                      +---------+---------+---------+---------
                    0.075     0.100     0.125     0.150
```

Figure 6.1   Average number of canceled orders each day of the week.

our study of the data we find that the average number of canceled orders for all Mondays is 0.08503 or 8.5% of total orders, and the average for Tuesdays is 12.4% (see Figure 6.1). The graph on the right shows the location of the average for the sample as a star. The actual average for the population will fall within the parentheses. These parentheses are wider for smaller samples because we are less sure of the actual population parameters when using a small sample. The parentheses are narrower when a larger sample has been studied. Friday's average is 14.4% of total, as is Thursday's.

The results indicate that Friday does have a high rate of cancellation. You can see, though, that Thursday is also high. In fact, the canceled order rate seems to increase through the week. So, this may be more than just a Friday problem. This is an important clue in analyzing the process. The question you'll want to ask is, "Why does the number of canceled orders increase during the course of a calendar week?"

Next, let's look at distributor type. This is a continuous output again, CO, and now we have only two categories of input, *end user* and *distributor*, so we will need to use the two-sample T-test. When we set up the data and analyze it, we see that the average and nearly all the data for E are much higher, as shown by the box plot, which is at a higher level than that of D (see Figure 6.2).

So, it is clear that the customers are the ones who cancel most of the orders, and distributors present only a fraction of the problem. This is also an important factor you'll want to study in order to reduce the overall number of canceled orders.

Now let's look at geographic region. Output is continuous with multiple categorized inputs, so what test shall we use? Yes—ANOVA; you are correct (see Figure 6.3).

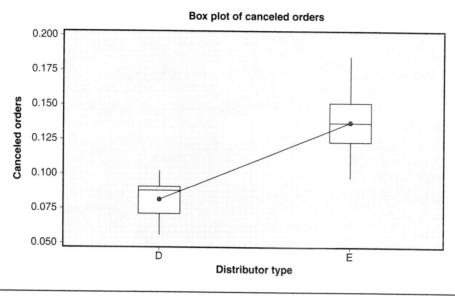

Figure 6.2   Comparison of orders canceled by distributors (D) and by end users/customers (E).

```
                         Individual 95% CIs For Mean
    Level   N    Mean    ---+---------+---------+---------+------
    1-NE    15   0.12285          (------*------)
    2-SE    15   0.12703               (------*------)
    3-MW    15   0.12280          (------*------)
    4-NE    15   0.12443            (-----*------)
    5-SW    15   0.12867                (------*-----)
                         ---+---------+---------+---------+------
                          0.110     0.120     0.130     0.140
```

Figure 6.3   ANOVA comparison of geographic regions.

When looking at the graph on the right side, a good rule of thumb is that if you can draw a vertical line through all of the confidence intervals (parentheses) then there is likely no difference between the variables.

There appears to be no real difference between the regions, even though we thought that the southwest was a bigger problem. It is just as important to understand which factors are not having an impact on the problem so that you do not waste time or make the problem worse by tampering with unbroken process elements.

To be sure, there is a higher rate of canceled orders in the southwest. It is not, however, a significantly higher level based on the sample of data you have collected. When we ran our sample size calculation, we said we wanted to be 95% confident, and that in order to be more confident, a larger sample would be needed. In other words, we can not be sure that next month the southwest will have the highest cancellation rate based on the data. And that's what we want, isn't it? We want to be able to predict your performance.

THE p-VALUE

There is a tool that will help us determine if a test result is statistically significant. This tool is the *p-value*, and it is a secondary result of every statistical hypothesis test. The p-value tells us, based on the sample we have analyzed and the results of that analysis, whether those results will hold true throughout the entire population, that is, beyond just that sample. The basic hypothesis of all our tests is that there is no difference from one category to the next. This is known as the *null hypothesis*—there is no difference. When we are testing our variables and looking for causes to our problems, then we are setting out to prove that there *is* a difference. This is the *alternate hypothesis*. In one of our examples—testing distributor versus end user for order cancellation rates—the null hypothesis of the test is that there is no difference: the cancellation rates are the same for both customer types. The alternate hypothesis is that there is a difference: one of the two has a higher cancellation rate. The detailed output table for customer type (Figure 6.4) shows that customers have a higher cancellation rate, and this is supported by the p-value of 0.000. The Green Belt's rule is that if you see a p-value less than 0.05, then you've found a significant variable. In statistical terms, such a low p-value means that you should reject the null hypothesis and you can believe that the alternate hypothesis is true. Remember that the cutoff for the p-value is 0.05 (not 0.50). The 0.05 comes from our confidence level of 95%, which is 0.95. It means that there is 5% or less of doubt about the test results. The day you find a low p-value is a good day because it means you can start fixing the root cause of your problem.

Let's return to our example and look at the *season* variable (see Figure 6.5). A vertical line can be drawn through all the intervals and not exclude any of them. You can see that the p-value is higher than 0.05. We accept the null hypothesis that there is no difference, specifically no difference in order cancellation rates between seasons.

Before we leave this section, let's look at the season variable another way. The number of canceled orders, as we discussed, is not a continuous variable because you can not cancel one half or three tenths of a product. In our scenario, you cancel a full order. Looking at the data in Figure 6.5, no one season shows a level of order cancellation that is significantly higher than the others. So why did we think summer was lower? Let's look at two variables together to see what might be happening (Figure 6.6). Looking at the number of orders canceled for each product during each season, we see that product

```
Two-sample T for Canceled

DistType    Mean    StDev
D          0.0807  0.0129
E          0.1372  0.0201

P-Value = 0.000
```

Figure 6.4   Details for the box plot shown in Figure 6.2 for customer type.

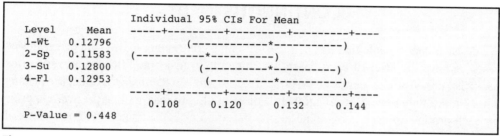

```
                    Individual 95% CIs For Mean
    Level     Mean   -----+---------+---------+---------+----
    1-Wt    0.12796                  (------------*-----------)
    2-Sp    0.11583   (-----------*-----------)
    3-Su    0.12800             (-----------*-----------)
    4-Fl    0.12953            (----------*-----------)
                      -----+---------+---------+---------+----
                       0.108     0.120     0.132     0.144
    P-Value = 0.448
```

Figure 6.5   Output table for season variable.

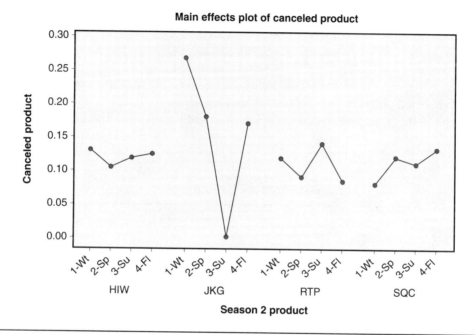

Figure 6.6   Comparing season (1, 2, 3, 4) and product code. Notice how most products are canceled at a consistent rate season to season except JKG, which is not canceled at all in summer and is canceled with greater frequency than the other products during winter, spring, and fall.

JKG is not canceled during the summer and is canceled with greater frequency in winter. In fact, it is the most highly canceled product of all and it's not canceled at all for three months of the year! This analysis gives us more direction in finding the causes of the problem because there is an obvious difference in the cancellation rate of JKG depending on the season. The project team must find out what is different and then try to 1) replicate the process that is in place during summer because it is good to have no cancellations, and 2) avoid the problems that JKG faces in the other seasons, especially winter.

CONTINUOUS INPUT

We do have one variable that can be measured on a continuous scale—the price. In this case, we have the price of each order, which can be transformed into an average price per order, per customer, per product, or per region, and can be made to reflect the pricing among more than one of those variables. For example, we may look at the average price for each product in each geographic region based on customer type, or we may look at average price of canceled orders during each season of the year. Don't hesitate to slice and sort your data in many ways—it can be very revealing.

Let's analyze the *price* variable against canceled order rate. To do this, we will need the statistical test that compares a continuous input and a continuous output—regression analysis. The purpose of our test is to see if a change in price causes a change in the order cancellation rate. When we set up the regression analysis, we see that an increase in price seems to lead to an increase in CO rate (see Figure 6.7). The solid line in the middle of the scatter diagram shows the prediction equation, meaning that you can determine the rate of canceled orders based on price by moving across the graph to that price and up the graph to the fitted line. When the points are tightly clustered close to the fitted line,

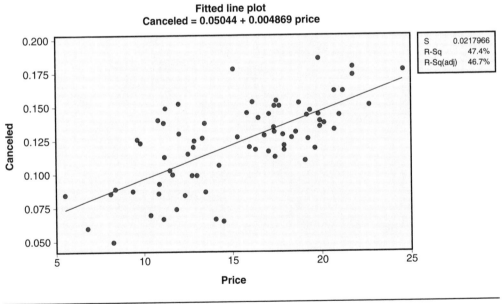

Figure 6.7   Regression analysis of canceled orders versus price to see whether there is a relationship. The solid line amid all the data points is drawn based on the calculated regression equation: Canceled orders = 0.05044 + (0.004869 times price). This is evidence of a positive relationship, meaning that as price increases, the number of canceled orders generally increases.

then the data are said to be highly correlated, and the prediction equation is very accurate and useful. When the points are less tightly clustered, the prediction equation is less accurate. The next step in this analysis would be to test the impact of price on order cancellations for each of the four product types to see if any specific product shows a stronger relationship of canceled orders to higher prices.

STATISTICAL PROBLEM INTO
STATISTICAL SOLUTION

So, what does all of this tell us? We have identified the conditions under which order cancellation rates are high and low, so now we have to take action to find out exactly why the problems are occurring. Is it enough to say, "Order cancellation rate is higher among end user customers than distributors, and it is highest with product JKG in seasons other than summer"? Or, if you continue to dig and analyze the data in more detail, would it be more useful to say, "Order cancellation rates are highest when customers Delta and Epsilon order product JKG at the end of Q1 and Q2 after hearing that distributor Gamma places a large replenishment order for JKG"? Digging into the input, process, and output variables will enable you to make such an exact determination of the who, what, when, where, and why of the problem.

STATISTICAL SOLUTION INTO
BUSINESS SOLUTION

Once you know the specific problem and its conditions, you can just tell the team not to accept large orders from Delta and Epsilon in January and April, right? Well, it may not be that simple.

A study conducted by a trucking firm found that miles per gallon (mpg) was improved by keeping tire pressure at 110 psi and keeping the vehicle's top speed to 55 miles per hour. This was the result of a statistical experiment conducted with a well-structured sampling plan and sufficient sample size under real conditions, so it was statistically valid. So, the next step was obviously to enforce both of those requirements. First, tire pressure. Drivers and maintenance crews were instructed to check all tires every time the vehicle took fuel, so that implementation was easy. On the top speed issue, though, there was a problem. When the truck drivers were told they'd be restricted to 55 mph, they threatened to quit because that is just too slow to get home at a reasonable hour, and because everyone, including dump trucks, would be passing them on the highways. Compromise was reached, and the top speed was reduced from 70 mph to 65 mph. This is an example of translating the statistical solution back into a business solution. Successful implementation of a tested solution is sometimes less about statistics and more about leadership.

In any case, now is the time to translate what we have learned through statistical analysis into the right recipe for the business. In Chapter 7 we will develop our solutions using lean tools and other techniques, and we will test them to make sure they work.

SUMMARY OF STATISTICAL ANALYSIS

1. You are translating the business problem into a statistical problem, finding the statistical solution, then translating that solution back into a business solution. During statistical analysis, you view the data only as x and y; there are no personalities or opinions involved.

2. Continuous data will be more powerful than discrete data because it provides more detail on the process and more insight into variation and the causes of defects. It should be used whenever possible. Instead of yes or no answers for meeting the customer's requirements, find a way to measure how well you achieved those objectives in continuous terms.

3. The steps in statistical analysis are:

    a. Test first to see if the data set is in control. Use a control chart. Don't test data that are not in control because the conclusions you draw can be faulty.

    b. Check to see that the data set is normally distributed. Many of the tests we are using assume a normally distributed data set and may not be robust for nonnormal data.

    c. If testing two or more data sets against each other, check to see if they exhibit a similar amount of variation. Testing a very tightly distributed data set against one that shows great variation can lead to inaccurate conclusions.

    d. Choose the right test for the job based on continuous or discrete inputs and outputs.

    e. All that being said, go out and challenge yourself to test your data, draw conclusions, test your conclusions, and make some improvements!

COACHING IMPROVEMENT PROJECTS

Enclosed with this book is a set of tools on CD for your use. All the tests in this chapter are included. Still, it is important to know where you can get help. The Six Sigma Green Belt is the intended reader of this book. Many organizations have put into place a number of experts who can help the Green Belt with project leadership. Black Belts, some of whom work full time on projects, are your first-choice resource for coaching. If your organization has one or more Master Black Belts, these experts are skilled at leading projects, coaching other project leaders, identifying new projects, implementing programs, and serving as an ambassador of process improvement to senior leaders. A parent or sister organization may have Lean Six Sigma experts with whom you can consult. Or your organization may have contracted with a Six Sigma consultant who can guide your project leadership. While it is a good idea to challenge yourself to do as much as you can, the success of a project depends in great part on the correct use of the tools provided. Ask for help when you need it.

Part IV

Improve

7

Develop and Test Your Improvements

Your process improvement project has been very well executed up to this point. To begin, you developed a charter that told everyone why the project is important and what your goals were. You made sure the scope of the project was not too large to be accomplished, and that you had the right team in place to give the project the best chance of success.

Next, you mapped your process so that everyone knew exactly what they were facing. That process map also showed you a number of important things. First, you saw who was involved at what phases of the process, which is helpful in identifying who needs to be involved in the improvements. You also looked for easy fixes or quick wins that could be addressed right away—things like unnecessary handoffs, non-value-adding steps, and approvals that were never disapproved and could be eliminated. Finally, the process map showed you the variables that needed to be listed for data collection—the input, process, and output variables that you would measure during and, in some cases, after the project.

You collected the necessary types and amounts of data based on your data collection plan and sampling strategy. It took you less than 30 days to collect data for the study because you wrote such a good data collection plan, and you didn't have to go back and ask people to collect more data for you because you didn't leave out any variables. It's much better to collect too much than not enough when you want to get your project done in ninety days.

Your team studied the process in pursuit of possible causes of defects, variation, delays, and other problems using process analysis, data analysis, and graphical analysis. Process analysis using the fishbone diagram and 5 whys technique led you to possible root causes of the problems. Data analysis validated or disproved those possible causes, and graphs helped you to see the data more clearly.

Then you wrote a recipe based on your analysis that would lead you to the best possible results in your process. Moving the critical variables in the direction that they need to go, and moving other variables to the level where they cost the least, has pointed you toward a very successful outcome from your improvement project.

Now that you have identified and verified the causes of your problems, it is time to fix them. And in order to fix them, you will test our solutions to make sure they address the problems and that they do not cause any unintended consequences, you will institutionalize them so that they become the new process for everybody every time, and you will measure them on an ongoing basis to make sure the improvement is sustained. So, let's get started!

There are many ways to make improvements now that the causes have been proven:

- Some solutions will be as simple as "Stop doing H, and start doing J."

- Others might involve some operator-level work instruction changes that may take a little time to adopt.

- Some solutions might require a disciplined approach to lean thinking in order to be realized.

- And some solutions will need an experiment before you can really prove that they will work as you want them to.

In any case, you will want to test the improvement during and after the solution is implemented. A very helpful tool for measuring the effectiveness of a solution is the *failure modes and effects analysis* (FMEA).

There are two main types of FMEA: the *process FMEA* (PFMEA) and the *design FMEA* (DFMEA). The DFMEA is used for a new product or process in order to launch it correctly the first time and identify necessary adjustments quickly. As such, it is a very strong tool for innovation and would really help any process improvements that are needed later by enabling the team to link the current process to the original assumptions. Since your project is a process improvement project and the process already existed before you began, we will assume that a DFMEA was not available when you started the project. The PFMEA is used to analyze a process step by step, listing all the possible problems that can happen while the process is being performed, listing all the possible causes for each of those problems, and calculating how big a problem each one is. We'll refer to this tool as the FMEA for our discussion.

The FMEA has been used since the 1940s to help organizations mitigate the risk of errors or failures in processes as critical as delivering an infant and as sensitive as lunar landings. Like all good risk analysis tools, it includes a measure of the frequency of the problem, which is called *occurrence*. Problems that happen more often are more important to correct.

Sample scale for occurrence:

1—Happens once a year or less

2—Happens once or twice a year

3—Happens three to five times per year or every other month

4—Happens monthly

5—Happens twice per month

6—Happens weekly

7—Happens more than once each week

8—Happens daily

9—Happens more than once per day

10—Happens all the time

This scale can be adapted for your organization's specific timing.

The FMEA also has a measure of the *severity* of the problem. Problems that cause more damage are more important to correct.

Sample scale for severity:

1—Little to no impact on customers or staff

2—Minor impact on performance, noticed by few

3—Overcome easily

4—Some performance loss is noticed

5—Could result in a complaint

6—Noticeable failure during use or during service

7—Significant customer dissatisfaction

8—Product or service unfit for use

9—Recall or service recovery needed

10—Causes injury to customer or employee

This scale can be adapted for your organization's specific conditions.

Just putting these two measures together can be very revealing. Which would you fix first: a problem that happens every week and causes only a nuisance to one or two people, or a problem that happens twice a year and causes devastation among your staff and customers?

The real strength of the FMEA, though, is its third calculation—*detectability*. This is the measure of how quickly you become aware of the problem after it has taken place. A problem that is easily detectable is one that you notice as soon as it happens. A problem with a high detectability score is one that you do not notice until after it has reached your customer or the end user and you have to find a way to stop it from reaching more of them.

Sample scale for detection:

1—Defect is obvious immediately

2—Automatic inspection is in place

3—100% inspection follows any indication of failure

4—Control/response plan is in place

5—Manual inspection for out-of-control indicators

6—Manual inspection for all units

7—Manual inspection for all units because failure is common

8—Manual inspection for all units based on a sampling plan

9—Occasional checks are in place, defects often slip through

10—Defect is not detectable until it reaches the customers

This scale can be adapted for your organization's specific processes.

Now, these three scores together will give you a very good idea of which problems to correct most urgently. When multiplied together, the three measures produce a *risk priority number* (RPN), and the highest numbers are the most important failure modes for the team to address.

Figure 7.1 shows a sample process FMEA created for insurance rate changes. Notice that one process step can have more than one failure mode, and each failure mode can have more than one cause.

There is more work to do with the tool after calculating the RPN. The right side of the FMEA is used for listing the steps that the team will take to reduce, eliminate, or mitigate the causes of each failure mode that is being addressed. Like a Pareto analysis, the highest RPNs will be handled first, those RPNs will be recalculated, and a new set of failure modes will move to the top of the list.

Figure 7.2 shows two Pareto charts: one for defects sorted by frequency and the second with the same defects sorted based on the cost to repair each one. The chart on top shows drips and runs as the most prevalent. When comparing the cost to repair each (a measure of severity), color and coverage move to the top of the list. Which problems would you address first?

The process FMEA is a very good tool to use on an ongoing basis to evaluate the key processes in an organization. It is certainly a useful tool to use during an improvement project because you can construct the FMEA while studying the process in the measure and analyze phases and then revise it after the improvements have been made. It will provide a comprehensive list of defects, causes, and solutions on a quantifiable scale. This is very compelling evidence of success from your project.

LEAN THINKING

There are volumes that have been written about *Lean Thinking*, starting with the original text from James Womack in 1991. There are a few primary tools from lean thinking that will be helpful during the improve phase of our project. These tools line up in a sequence that is most easily described in a factory setting, but can be translated into any workplace—factory or otherwise:

1. 5S is an important first step in the development of a continuous improvement culture because its primary focus is on each individual. The 5S formula is foundational because it starts with keeping one's own work space clean,

Process/Product
Failure Modes and Effects Analysis (FMEA)

Process or product name:	Implement new insurance rates for states in category 4					Prepared by: José G.		Page 1 of 1	
Responsible:	Process owner—Mitch M.					FMEA date (orig) Aug. 20, 2010		(rev)	

Process step/input	Potential failure mode	Potential failure effects	Sev	Potential causes	Occ	Current controls	Det	RPN	Actions recommended
What is the process step/ input under investigation?	In what ways does the key input go wrong?	What is the impact on the key output variables (customer requirements) or internal requirements?	How severe is the effect to the customer?	What causes the key input to go wrong?	How often does cause or FM occur?	What are the existing controls and procedures (inspection and test) that prevent either the cause or the failure mode? Should include an SOP number.	How well can you detect cause or FM?		What are the actions for reducing the occurrence of the cause, or improving detection? Should have actions only on high RPNs or easy fixes.
Update rate table	Headline information inaccurate	New rate table will not be accepted by the system	1	Typing errors	2	Peer and manager review	2	4	None required
Update rate table	New calculated rates are inaccurate	Customer's new billing statement will be incorrect	9	Typing errors	4	Post-implementation review of sample policies	5	180	Implement early warning report
Update rate table	New calculated rates are inaccurate	Customer's new billing statement will be incorrect	9	Failure to identify underwriting interactions	6	Post-implementation review of sample policies	5	270	Implement early warning report
Test sample policies	Fail to find mistakes	Customer's new billing statement will be incorrect	9	Insufficient sample size	4	SOP for sample size calculation and process	3	108	Categorize sample size calculation
Move rates into production	System update does not occur	New rate table will not be accepted by the system	1	Too many implementations in one night	2	Move up scheduling SOP	2	4	None required
Print output and send	Printing process not completed	Updated policy not mailed to customer same day	6	Overload or outage in print room	2	Preventive maintenance SOP	2	24	None required

Figure 7.1 Sample process FMEA created for insurance rate changes. Notice that one process step can have more than one failure mode, and each failure mode can have more than one cause.

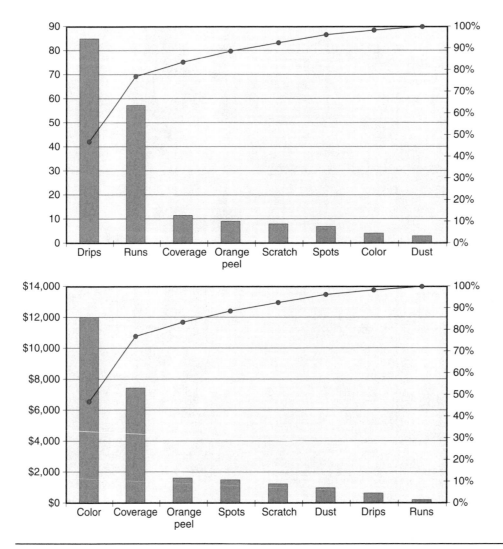

Figure 7.2 Two Pareto charts of the same paint defects sorted differently.

organized, easy to use, and safe. The five words that begin with S were originally Japanese, but they've been adapted to English for widespread use. They are:

- *Sort* (*seiri* in Japanese). The tools or materials that you need most often should be closest to you, and those that are used less often should be stored farther away or even in a central location. An example of *sort* is the Russian typewriter keyboard. While the western nations tend to use the QWERTY keyboard, which allows all fingers to be used frequently throughout the process of typing, the Russian keyboard concentrates the letters that are used most often in that language around the index fingers and moves outward from there based on frequency of use. The assumption is that the fingers on the hand become less accurate as you move toward your pinkies! Another good example of *sort* is to assemble a toolkit for specific jobs and, when that job arises, you go get the toolkit that is labeled for that job, rather than keeping all those tools in your work space.

- *Set in order (seiton)*. There is a place for everything, and everything is in its place. Once you've decided what needs to be stored in what location, make sure it is always there, always available when you need it, and always returned to its specific location. A good example of *set in order* is drawing the outline of a wrench or hammer on a pegboard above someone's workbench in the garage. If you've ever reached for the stapler and it's not there, you're a victim of faulty *seiton*!

- *Shine (seiso)*. Clean everything as you use it, and there will not be a time when the item you use is not clean. Whether it's a tool in a factory, a database in a bank, a list of customers, or a website, if it's not clean and up to date, then it may not be working as well as it could. Waste is caused when you have to stop what you are doing to check if the tools you are using are capable of doing the job.

- *Standardize (seiketsu)*. Keep the process going all the time. The first three steps must be employed regularly, without fail, and each individual is responsible for his or her own area. In addition, the managers, peers, and other areas of the organization will watch to make sure each person is living up to the agreement to keep the 5S culture living. If I were writing the English translations for the Japanese 5S words, I might choose "schedule" for the fourth step, so everyone would know what is expected and when to do it.

- *Sustain (shitsuke)*. Pass your success along, share your success stories with others, and reward success of the 5S program. Use tools like recognition, storyboard communication, published stories of time and energy saved, and praise to make sure everyone knows this is a useful set of tools.

2. *Visual factory*. Once each person has achieved 5S, the whole plant can live up to the same expectation of organized behavior. A visual factory is not only one where everything that is made in each department is labeled for easy identification, it is also a workplace where information about performance is easily accessible by those who need it, on and off the factory floor.

3. *Kanban*. Now that everyone knows what can be expected of everybody else and where to find every process, just-in-time replenishment and one-piece flow can be implemented to save time, cost, rework, and waste.

4. *Kaizen.* When the factory is organized into a flow, you will begin to uncover specific problems that need to be fixed. These problems will move around the factory floor, and each one should be addressed with a *kaizen event.* After everyone has been involved with at least one kaizen event, they will become skilled in finding and making improvements without being asked.

5. *Six Sigma DMAIC.* Some projects will not be easily solved with a three- or four-day kaizen event. They will require additional study, data analysis, and pilot testing. At this point, the culture of the organization is to make improvements as a team and not to take anything personally. This environment is ripe for well-scoped DMAIC projects to be successful (in ninety days!). Note that lean thinking can lead to Six Sigma projects, and Six Sigma projects can call for the use of lean in developing solutions. The two tool sets really do work well together.

6. *Design for Six Sigma.* Any new venture will be studied in order to get it right the first time. "Launch and learn" is a thing of the past.

This progression, when followed in order, will give your organization a better chance of creating sustainable change. Skipping a level or two may bring success with the right team at the right time. From what I have seen, the most thorough, penetrating, and lasting approach is the disciplined one shown here.

So, how does this set of tools become useful in the *improve* phase of your project? You may find, through the course of the project, that steps in the evolution have been skipped, and it is necessary to go back and 5S one or more work areas to avoid problems that are being caused during the process.

You may find that the cycle time of your process—be it a production and assembly shop, a transactional back office, a customer-facing service, or anywhere else—can be improved by establishing a team that is capable of working on a variety of processes and then putting only the type of service or product that is needed at that time through the process. You could find that your overall cost can be reduced dramatically by pulling through the process only the products and services that are required, and only when they are needed and not sooner. Both of these are examples of using one-piece flow to produce only what is necessary and no more: no batches or minimum order quantities. This can improve your relationship with your customer as well.

PILOT TESTING

Improvements, when identified, need to be tested. There are two primary objectives for any pilot test. The first is to prove that your solution will work. The second is to uncover any unintended consequences that might arise as a result of the solution. Let's look at the second objective first.

Unintended consequences of your process improvement can create problems in another process or another area of the organization. A very instructive example is

Lean Thinking

The goal of lean thinking is to reduce waste in your process as much as you possibly can so that you spend the minimum amount of time and expense to make the product or provide the service that your customer needs. When talking about what your customer needs or wants, it is really a question of value. There are many definitions for "value" available. In its most basic form, it is this:

$$Value = Benefit - Cost$$

In other words, the customer gets value when the usefulness, worth, or benefit of the product or service being purchased exceeds the price he paid for it. For our purpose in discussing process improvement, customer value means the parts of your process that the customer is willing to pay for. Picture yourself giving your customers a tour of your work area. You would probably be very proud to show them the production areas: "Welcome to the belt factory. This is where we cut the leather into strips. This is where we add holes to adjust the length of the belt. Over there is where we treat the leather with our patented stain-resistant coating, and behind that is where we test a sample of the belts. And finally, here is where we add the buckles." You might be less likely to find yourself saying, "Here is where we store the buckets of stain-resistant coating, this is where we file paperwork, and that is our production scheduling room." While things like production scheduling, storage, and filing may be very important for internal purposes to your organization, they are not usually important to your customer.

As we've discussed, every process is made up of steps. Some of the steps in the process will go directly toward providing value to the customer, some steps will be necessary for your organization although they do not generate customer value, and some steps being conducted today may provide no value at all. We will use the lean approach to identify these non-value-adding steps, to identify waste in the process, and to reduce or eliminate both.

There are really five steps in the overall lean approach to doing business. The key words are value, value stream, flow, pull, and perfection.

1. Identify the value. What is the customer really willing to pay for?

2. Map the value stream. And don't just map it; make sure you are looking for ways to improve it all along the way. Any step in the process that does not actually create value needs to be examined closely for removal.

3. Once you have specified all the necessary steps in creating the value that your customer needs, arrange the sequence of work so that the product or service being created will flow uninterrupted and quickly to the customer.

4. When the flow of the process is thus arranged, allow your customer's demand to pull the materials and services through the process only when they are needed. Don't push, you will only create waste.

5. Every time the process is executed, look for ways to improve—every time. This is striving for perfection, a goal that is difficult to reach, yet wonderful to pursue. Perfection would be a process with absolutely no waste created at all.

Continued

Continued

So, how will you apply lean thinking to your project and with the concepts presented in this book? You will likely find that the tools in lean work very well in a few main areas. First, at the very beginning of the project, one of the most important discussions the team and sponsor will have is the preparation of the project charter and its six sections. Of those six, the business case, the problem statement, the scope, and the goal statement must all directly reflect the value that the customer gets from the process that is targeted for improvement. Identifying that value correctly is critical to project success. If the output of the process is not of value to the customer, there must be another compelling reason for executing that process or else it is not a good use of your time.

Next, in the early stages of the project, the process will be mapped. Flowcharting is very good, and value stream mapping can be even better for showing opportunities to improve and to eliminate waste. Those quick wins your team will find will often be a result of looking through the lens of lean.

Later in the project you will have found the root causes of variation and defects, and it will be time to make improvements. Lean thinking will help you streamline process steps, regroup and re-sequence the process to reduce time and defects, and level the work load so the team is able to produce as much output as possible with as few resources as possible.

Finally, once the process has been improved, those improvements will need to be sustained. Striving for perfection by continually reviewing, analyzing, and looking for improvements is a cultural change that is not easily achieved but is highly effective while it's being chased.

the team that identified a chronic failure to deliver products to customers on time. The team's solution was to use a different shipping method. On-time delivery improved, and the team celebrated. Meanwhile, in the finance office, questions were coming fast about why the cost of expedited freight was rising through the roof. One arrow goes down, another goes up (see Figure 7.3). This X shape is the shape of unintended consequences. The team should have looked for a way to produce the product better and faster, not a way to ship faster the product that was manufactured slowly!

What sorts of unintended consequences can show up during pilot testing? One of the original questions raised in this book will help with that answer: "speed, accuracy, or cost?" If you have improved the speed of the process, has there been an increase in defects or cost? If you have improved accuracy, has that resulted in a slower process, or one that costs more to perform? And if you have cut the costs, has this resulted in less accuracy, or a less timely process? There are other unintended consequences you may experience that are specific to your organization and its customers, employees, and other stakeholders. The story from Chapter 6 about the truck drivers who refused to drive 55 miles per hour comes to mind.

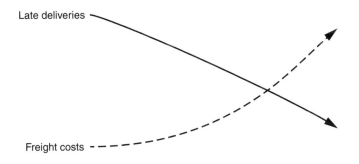

Figure 7.3   Late deliveries trend downward, while expedited freight cost increases.

An excellent way to identify unintended consequences through pilot testing is to run the new process in the real world. You may create a safe environment to do that, and it's sensible to do so. You must remember to include in the test as many adjacent and concurrent processes as you can so that you will get the best possible idea of how your improvements will affect the rest of the organization. Market testing of new restaurant products to see how customers react is a great way to pilot new menu items, just in case they don't work. Launching a beta version of a website can help an organization identify software incompatibilities. Choosing one country to make a process change for a month or two can reveal shortcomings in the plan and help to refine details.

PROVING THE SOLUTION

Your other main objective is to prove that your solution really works! This is going to require planning and attention from the project manager and team. If the pilot test is not well organized, and if the team does not stay engaged during the test period, the ninety-day goal for project completion can be missed. This is because the observations made during the pilot test are critical in refining the solution for full implementation, and they can only be learned by being present during the test.

Now, it is also possible to be *too* present during the pilot test. If your project team does all the work that normally would be done by somebody else, then you might not get a fair representation of how the improved process will work. Further, even if the real process owners and operators are performing the process during the test, if the project team is watching them too closely they might not behave as they normally would when you're not watching. A balance must be struck, and this balance is achieved through detailed planning.

What should the pilot test plan look like? A few key pieces of information will need to be included (see Table 7.1). After that, it's up to you and your team to make any additional plans that will be helpful to your organization.

Some pilot tests are more stressful than others. Taking the time to plan in advance will help to ensure the success of the test, the improved process, and the project.

Table 7.1   Pilot test considerations.

1	New process map	Including detailed work instructions	
2	Data collection plan for the test	What data will we need to prove that the process works?	Include MSA
3	Who will perform the process?	What training will be needed in advance?	Prepare a pretest briefing
4	Expected results	What unexpected consequences did we encounter?	Brief adjacent functional teams
5	Evaluation of test	How and when will we evaluate the pilot test?	

Team Meeting #4

Plan a Full Day for Team Meeting #4

After reviewing the findings of the root cause analysis, improvement plans are discussed. It is helpful to give the root cause information to the team members a few days prior to meeting #4 so they can think about possible solutions and bring those ideas into the meeting.

The team can list possible solutions to the specific problems identified based on the validated root causes of those problems. Discussion of possible solutions is useful because one good idea can build on others and turn into a plan that will accomplish the objectives and also build enthusiasm for the improved process. It is also important to uncover any possible unintended consequences of the improvements that are being discussed.

The team will agree on a pilot plan for the improvements and prepare a pilot test plan including the items shown in Table 7.1.

Meeting #5 will follow meeting #4 by two weeks, during which time the pilot test will be conducted. The project leader will also have a few more things to do before meeting #5, and it would be very useful to delegate assignments to team members in order to balance the workload and stay on track with project completion in ninety days. One is to prepare the cost/benefit analysis (Chapter 8) after the pilot test has been completed, and the other is to prepare a draft control/response plan (Chapter 9).

8
Cost/Benefit Analysis

One of the objectives of a process improvement project is to save money for the organization. Most projects will bring with them tangible monetary benefits resulting from decreased cost, improved delivery speed, and fewer defects requiring rework or warranty expense. Nearly all projects will produce intangible benefits like ease of doing business, better teamwork, and improved morale. Benefits, when listed and quantified, really support the use and continuation of a Lean Six Sigma program. And if the organization is able to sell the program as a differentiator among its competitors, successful projects can also lead to an increase in revenue, which makes even more stakeholders happy.

In order to complete the project and produce the projected benefits, costs will sometimes be incurred by the project team. Starting from the beginning, the time required to have the five team meetings and to do the work in between costs the company money, testing the process and destructive sampling can take place and bring costs, the purchase of a statistical software package may be desirable for calculations, a small celebration at the project's completion can bring a little expense with it, and a Six Sigma consultant or trainer may seem like a good investment in the early days of the program. In addition, the actual solution that is generated by the project team may add cost if it means a change in machinery, personnel responsibilities, software and reporting, maintenance, cleaning, scheduling, or training.

It will be very important to accurately report the costs associated with the improvement and compare them to the benefits that will be realized over the course of a year. This will serve two main purposes: first, to support the implementation of the solution when the benefit outweighs the cost, and second, to capture the benefit of each project and add it to the full benefit of all lean and Six Sigma projects in the entire portfolio, thus evaluating financially the effectiveness of the program. There are many ways to show costs and benefits to a review panel and to others in the organization. Here are a few.

COST/BENEFIT TEMPLATE

To list all the benefits on one side of a page and all the costs on the other, with sums at the bottom of each column, is the simplest way to show whether benefits exceed costs (see Table 8.1).

Table 8.1   Side-by-side cost/benefit table.

Project costs	Project benefits	Intangible benefits	Net result
Meetings and supplies $4,850	Decreased rework $40,500	Decrease in customer complaints	
Revised process $23,730	Reduced warranty costs $13,380		Savings of $25,300

There may be some specifics in the way your organization wants to see costs and benefits shown. It will likely be some variation of Table 8.1.

Your organization may prefer to see a calculation of the financial impact of the project over time. Calculations like net present value and return on investment have been very useful in securing approval for improvement projects and the solutions they identify. *Net present value* (NPV) is a measure of a series of cash flows in the future: you will save a certain amount of money each year based on the improvements you made through your project, so you'll calculate what that is worth to the company today considering gross savings, interest, and the expected duration of the savings. *Return on investment* (ROI) is simply a ratio of the benefit received to the cost incurred from an investment, and is usually expressed as a percentage: $90 gained, $45 spent, ROI = 2:1 or 200%.

ACTIVITY-BASED COSTING

Another useful way to show the actual benefits of a process improvement project comes under the heading of *activity-based management* or *activity-based costing* (ABC). Costs can be categorized into general buckets: fixed and variable; costs of manufacturing, selling, distribution, and administration; direct and indirect; and more. It can be very difficult for a diverse organization to capture accurate information about its costs. What are the chances you'll get them all correct? What assurance do you have that the calculated costs today will be the same tomorrow? And what will you do with all that information anyway? People can not really manage costs—they must manage the activities that cause the costs.

One of the central principles of ABC is that it is better to be approximately right about your costs than to be totally wrong. For this reason, ABC does not insist on detailing every single cost. Instead, you will identify the main costs you incur and trace them to their sources. We'll need to introduce some terms:

Direct costs: Those costs that are incurred in the production of a finished product or service, for example, the materials and labor used in manufacturing.

Indirect costs: Often called "overhead," these are costs that are not directly tied to the finished product. Examples are business support services, administrative costs, and heating the building.

Activities: The value-adding processes that transform inputs into outputs that the customer will pay for.

Cost driver: The factor that determines the amount of money consumed during the performance of an activity. Usually it is the quantity of work that determines how many times the activity has to be performed.

Object: The result of the process, that is, the output of the process that the customer is buying.

Here is how the process works:

1. Identify the cost you want to study.

2. If the cost is direct, trace it to the object produced. The cost driver will be the number of objects produced.

3. Trace indirect or overhead costs to the activity that generates the cost. The cost driver will be the number of times the activity has to be performed.

4. Calculate the cost per cost driver.

5. Now challenge the need to perform the activity, and look for ways to reduce the cost per cost driver.

6. Eliminate the activity, if possible, or find ways to improve the process.

Let's look at a couple of examples (see Figure 8.1), using horizontal analysis (left to right). In the recruitment (indirect) example, the next step for the team will be to analyze the process for posting open positions in search of reduced cost. When fewer ads have to be posted for less time, costs will abate. The team will also study the effectiveness

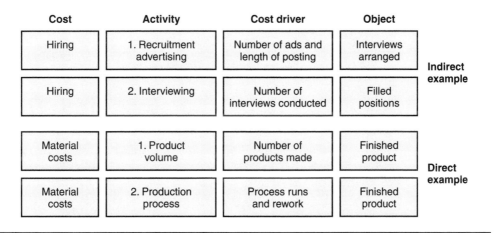

Figure 8.1   Indirect and direct activity-based costing examples.

of interviewing techniques and the entire interviewing process to minimize the expense associated with getting the best person into the job. When the team is able to interview fewer candidates to find the right person, costs will also be reduced.

In the factory (direct) example, the team will study the scheduling, batch size, and rework in order to reduce overall material costs.

In a previous paragraph I stated that people can not really control costs, only the activities that drive those costs. I do not mean to take away any importance from the roles of purchasing and supplier management. If you are able to negotiate a better price, that is usually a very good thing for the firm. For our purposes, we are talking about process improvement and not negotiation.

There are two very important similarities between ABC and Lean Six Sigma as it has been described in this book. The first is found in the horizontal analysis. Notice the left-to-right structure of the cost analysis. Moving from the listed cost, through the activity and cost driver, to the object is really a parallel to our process mapping framework:

$$\text{Input} \to \text{Process} \to \text{Output}$$

This is also similar to the discussion during preparation of your data collection plan: you measure input variables, process variables, and output variables to analyze the process comprehensively.

The second parallel is found in the approach to improving costs. You will study those specific costs that have the most impact on your overall cost first, rather than collect all information on all costs at once. This is very much like the Pareto principle: you look at the tallest bars on the Pareto chart to decide which factors to improve first because they will have the most impact.

When presented as a cost/benefit analysis, ABC will show the decision makers exactly how your team's solution will impact costs rather than outlining a general ballpark number. This can be very compelling when you are looking for approval of a new process improvement. You only have ninety days to make an impact, so study the costs that you can control.

Part V
Control

9

Control/Response Plan

When leading a project or delivering Six Sigma training, I am frequently asked, "What is the most important phase of a DMAIC project?" My answer has changed over the years. Early in my process improvement career I used to say that *analyze* was the most important because you have to find the real root cause of the problem and not just accept the popular belief. I changed my answer to *improve* while working in more transactional and service areas because the opportunities to make innovative improvements were abundant and interesting and because you really have to make an improvement that people will embrace and implement in order for it to work. Experience has shown me that *define* and *measure* are also critical because, as has been said, a project well started is only half done. *Define* is important because you could choose a project that is just too big to accomplish, and *measure* is important because you could extend the time required to complete a project by not preparing a good data collection plan.

Thus, all phases of the DMAIC project are important, for these and other reasons. However, my answer to the initial question, if you asked me today, would be *control*. After having seen and led so many projects, I can state with certainty that unless the project team fully institutionalizes the solutions and improvements, there is a good chance that the gains that were achieved during the project will be lost when the excitement of the project ends, the project team disbands, and the project leader moves on to the next assignment. Change can be difficult, and it can be very tempting to go back to the old way of doing things once the spotlight moves somewhere else and the attention dies down.

It is a common practice to track the benefits of a process improvement project for twelve months after those benefits begin to be realized. The objective of the control phase of your project is to make sure the process improvements that the team produces are implemented correctly and sustained. You will identify your improvements, document them clearly, put them into action everywhere they are required, establish the permanent data collection plan, and identify the steps that will be taken whenever the problem you just fixed appears again. In the end, you will have a *control and response plan* that will serve these purposes. It is divided into three parts:

1. New process map

2. Data collection plan for monitoring the ongoing process

3. Response plan for out-of-control indicators

Let's get started.

DOCUMENTING THE NEW PROCESS

In the define phase of your project, you prepared a process map showing the way the process worked at that time. This is known as the "as is" process map. Your new process with all of your improvements has taken shape throughout the analyze and improve phases and is called the "should be" or "to be" process map (see Figure 9.1). That is now the new process, and it will need to be documented for all current and future team members to follow.

The new process map, when completely drawn by the team, needs to be validated with the actual operators and managers of the functional area. One reason for this is to verify, as you did during the pilot test, that there is nothing in this process or any adjacent processes that will lead to unintended consequences. Another very good reason for this is to make sure that the process owners are involved in the decisions that affect their area of operation, both for practical purposes and in the pursuit of teamwork. When all the team members and process operators agree that the new process as documented is the way the work will be performed from now on, then old work instructions and process maps need to be thrown away (recycled!) and only the new process will be employed. Documenting this new process on your control/response plan is the next step toward institutionalizing your improvements (see Figure 9.2).

Our approach to measuring the new process will be based on the data collection plan you used during the project. From Chapter 3 we know that it is important to collect data from all parts of your process: inputs to the process, the process steps and variables, and outputs from the process. We agreed that it is better to collect data from many sources

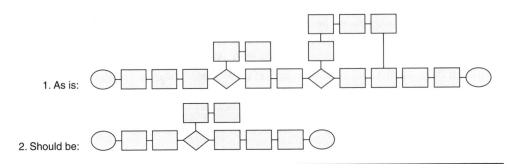

Figure 9.1   "As is" and "should be" process maps.

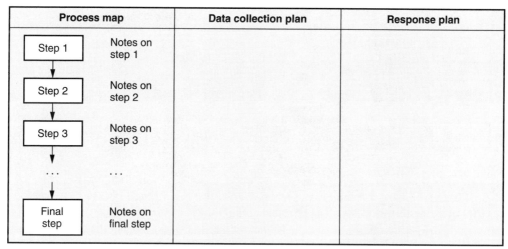

Figure 9.2   The new process map located on the left side of the control/response plan, including notes for performing the steps of the improved process.

than to go back later and ask the operators to collect more data for your project. As a result, your data collection plan may have started its life as a very long list of variables to study.

When you entered the analyze phase of the project, you were looking for the variables that would have the most impact on your process. It took some research and some patience, and you found your critical few variables. Maybe it was only one variable that made the difference, or maybe three. Whatever the number, they need to be measured from now on to make sure they stay where you want them to be. If you wanted variable $x1$ to be between 92 and 94, you'll need to measure it every time to make sure it stays within that band.

Of course, you'll continue to measure the output of the process, and maybe in the past that was the only measure you used. I have often heard that organizations are very good at measuring their delivery time, complaints, success rate or yield, pass/fail ratio, and profit. Now we can see that there is more that must be measured and that those outputs are the results of a process that has more variables in it that need to be tracked.

It's really not going to be that big a job measuring the new process. You'll track the process output and the critical few variables that you identified. You will add those to the control/response plan in the middle section (see Figure 9.3).

Remember that the data collection plan included several elements. In Chapter 3 we listed seven steps to collecting useful data, and you'll want to do the same here. First, you'll list *what* data are being collected and *how* you'll gather that information. For example, you will measure the time required to load each pallet of marketing materials completely, and you'll measure it with a stopwatch that is started when the conveyor belt starts and stopped when the last packing strap is tightened.

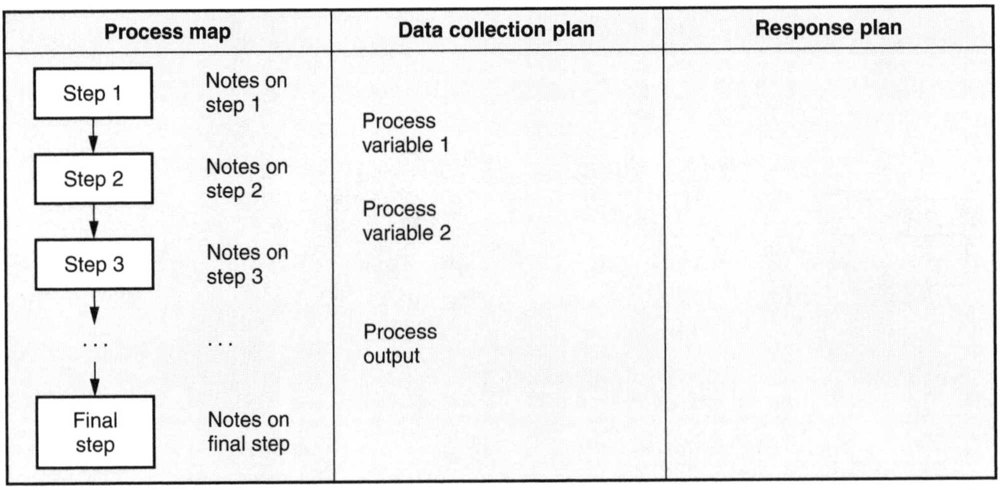

Process map		Data collection plan	Response plan
Step 1	Notes on step 1	Process variable 1	
Step 2	Notes on step 2	Process variable 2	
Step 3	Notes on step 3		
. . .	. . .	Process output	
Final step	Notes on final step		

Figure 9.3   Control/response plan with the names of the measures added. Next, you'll add the method for collecting data.

Next, you will make sure you have conducted measurement system analysis so that everyone collects the data the same way every time. When people are collecting data, it is important to error-proof the data collection process. When machines are recording data, it is still important to make sure they are doing it consistently. A machine of any sort can lose its accuracy over time or if it is shocked, and two or more machines can lose their calibration as well.

Your third step will be to keep the data collection process as simple as possible. Simple data collection sheets, time stamps, prefilled forms, and defined error codes are some ways to make sure the work of data collection is not too confusing or time-consuming to be executed consistently. Fourth and fifth, you will want to check on the data collection process occasionally to make sure it is being conducted properly, and spot-check the data to see if it matches expectations.

Sixth, use graphs and charts to show the data visually. We will present more on this step in the following section. The seventh step is to retain the data you have collected in case it is necessary to go back and check the data during a past period of time.

CONTROL CHARTS

We will introduce two more types of charts that can be helpful in the control phase of your project and during ongoing process management. These are known as *control charts*, and they help us to see the patterns of variation in the process. There are many types of control charts, and the choice of which chart to use depends on the data that are being collected. For the purpose of completing your ninety-day project, we will introduce only four charts: two for continuous data and two for discrete data. Remember that continuous data can be measured on a continuous scale, and discrete data can not.

CONTINUOUS DATA CONTROL CHARTS

The continuous data control charts will be used to track inputs or outputs that can be measured on a continuous scale. Examples of these include the time spent to complete a process, air pressure in pounds per square inch, the temperature of the air in a machine, dollars of marketing expense or revenue, and average handle time in a call center. You'll plot those data points one at a time from left to right on your chart like the time series plot we have previously discussed. Each individual value follows the previous value on the chart, and those two points are connected with a line. In addition to that line, we will add three more lines to create the control chart from the time series plot.

The first line to be added is the *mean*, or *average*, of all the points shown on the chart. It will be one dotted straight line at the value of the mean running the full width of the chart (see Figure 9.4).

This centerline will help you to see variation in the process. When speaking about the average of a process, you will expect that about half the points will be above the line and about half will be below it. When you see a cluster of points all above the line, this could be an indication that something is not right in the process.

Before you can really analyze the variation in your process, we will need to add the other two lines. These are the *control limits*, and they are calculated from the data. Just as we calculated the average in Figure 9.4, we will now determine the standard deviation, which equals 0.53. A tip for calculating standard deviation: in MS Excel, use {=STDEV(x:x)}. That number is then multiplied by three, and the resulting number is both added to and subtracted from the mean to calculate the value of the upper and lower control limits (UCL and LCL). See Figure 9.5.

The control limits are calculated this way because statistical probability defines the percentage of data points that will fall within plus or minus three standard deviations of

Data:
8.1, 7.6, 8.1, 7.8, 8.2,
7.0, 7.8, 7.0, 8.8, 7.8,
8.1, 7.1, 8.1, 7.1, 8.2

Average (mean):
7.79

Figure 9.4   Time series plot with centerline added at the mean of all the points.

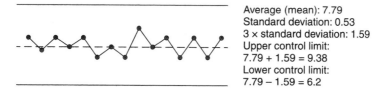

Average (mean): 7.79
Standard deviation: 0.53
3 × standard deviation: 1.59
Upper control limit:
7.79 + 1.59 = 9.38
Lower control limit:
7.79 − 1.59 = 6.2

Figure 9.5   Time series plot with upper (UCL) and lower (LCL) control limits added.

a centerline as 99.7% of the total in a normal distribution. Any point that falls above the UCL or below the LCL is a real exception, considering that only 0.15% of data points on either side can be in that zone. This doesn't mean that it's impossible for a point to lie outside the control limits. It just means that those points need to be investigated to find out what happened. Conversely, a point that is inside the control limits does not need to be investigated because it is not outside the expected range of data points.

Now that we have constructed the chart that shows the individual values of the variable, there is a second part of the control chart that is just as important. This will be the lower half of the overall chart page, and it will show the amount of variation in the top chart. There are two ways to depict this variation.

First, if individual values are being charted in the top chart, then the lower chart will show the absolute value of the change from one point to the next. For example, the time required to complete one driver's license exam at one computer terminal in the Bureau of Motor Vehicles is listed in the top chart in Figure 9.6. The individual values are listed from left to right showing the time required for each person to take the exam. The first time is five minutes, the second is six, and so on. The average is six minutes.

The difference from the first point (5) to the second point (6) is 1, so that is plotted at the far left of the *moving range chart* (bottom chart in Figure 9.6). The best thing to see on this chart is low numbers, as close to zero as possible, because that means there is little variation in the process.

A similar control chart will be used when the top chart is being used to track more than one individual value. As an example, suppose your team runs quality control checks of phone calls in a call center. Each of the seven members of your team will listen to a certain number of calls each hour. You want to track how many calls they are reviewing each hour. If you were to plot the number of calls reviewed by person 1 in the first hour, then person 2, then person 3, and so on for all seven, then plot person 1's calls for the second hour as point eight, you would not be plotting a continuous process. This would

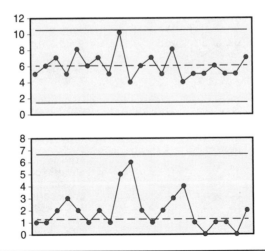

Figure 9.6　Individuals and moving range (I-MR) chart for continuous data.

not represent the team's performance as a unit. If you wanted to plot each person's productivity, you would need seven I-MR charts.

To show the team's performance, you'll use a chart that depicts the average and variation in calls reviewed among all seven team members each hour. The top half of this chart will show the team's average, which is labeled X-bar ($\bar{X}$), and the bottom chart will show the variation in that team's output for each hour. For variation we will typically use the standard deviation.

The data table for twenty hours of calls reviewed is shown in Table 9.1. The control chart would look like Figure 9.7.

The average output from all seven team members is plotted from left to right in the upper chart. The overall average is 6.3 calls and is shown by the dotted centerline. Notice the points above and below the control limits. These points indicate an unexpectedly high or low average.

The lower chart shows that within each hour there is variation in the number of calls each team member reviews. Less variation would produce a data point closer to

Table 9.1   Data table for twenty hours of reviewed calls.

	Dave	Tina	Lucy	Warren	Cliff	Ron	Mandy	Average	Std dev
Hour 1	6	7	6	3	5	6	5	5.4	1.3
Hour 2	7	9	6	4	6	6	7	6.4	1.5
Hour 3	6	11	6	5	6	6	5	6.4	2.1
Hour 4	6	10	7	5	5	6	7	6.6	1.7
Hour 5	7	7	6	3	5	6	7	5.9	1.5
Hour 6	5	8	6	4	6	6	8	6.1	1.5
Hour 7	4	9	7	4	6	6	7	6.1	1.8
Hour 8	5	9	7	3	5	6	5	5.7	1.9
Hour 9	6	6	6	6	5	6	6	5.9	0.4
Hour 10	7	10	7	5	6	6	6	6.7	1.6
Hour 11	7	12	6	5	6	6	5	6.7	2.4
Hour 12	8	11	6	4	7	7	7	7.1	2.1
Hour 13	7	9	6	6	6	6	5	6.4	1.3
Hour 14	5	9	7	3	7	6	8	6.4	2.0
Hour 15	3	10	6	4	6	6	6	5.9	2.2
Hour 16	4	8	7	4	5	6	6	5.7	1.5
Hour 17	6	9	7	3	5	6	6	6.0	1.8
Hour 18	7	11	7	5	6	7	13	8.0	2.9
Hour 19	7	12	6	4	6	7	6	6.9	2.5
Hour 20	8	8	6	5	5	6	7	6.4	1.3

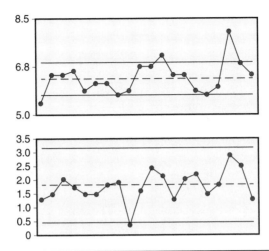

Figure 9.7 $\bar{X}$ and *s* chart for reviewed call data from Table 9.1 (continuous data).

zero. The one point that is below the control limit may be a good thing because it shows that the entire team was producing about the same output.

The next steps the team would take include examining the out-of-control points to find out what was different in the process during those hours. If someone reviewed a particularly high number of calls, what was the reason? Were they short calls? Was the person doing a thorough job? And if someone reviewed a number of calls that was smaller than usual, what was the reason for that? These specific issues will help the team to identify improvements that can be sustained.

DISCRETE DATA CONTROL CHARTS

Data not measured on a continuum are discrete. For practical purposes, this is usually a count of items or events: the number of defects, the number of complaints, the number of people interviewed, and other counted variables. We'll use some of the same calculations to prepare the control charts for discrete data. First of all, the upper chart will be produced exactly the way it was in the I-MR chart, by plotting the individual data points from left to right, adding the centerline that represents the average of the process, and adding upper and lower control limits based on three standard deviations above and below the centerline. The number of defects produced each day is plotted from left to right in this control chart, called a c-chart (see Figure 9.8).

Over the full period of the study the defects are categorized to see which problems are most significant. Just as we did with the continuous data control charts, we will add a second chart to the bottom. In this case, a pie chart is used.

Since we are dealing with counted events and not continuous data, finding clues to solve our problem depends heavily on studying the details about the defects themselves.

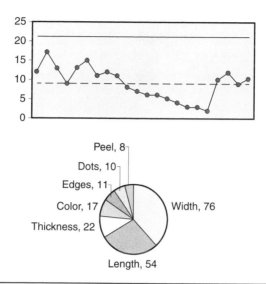

Figure 9.8   Discrete data plotted in c-chart with accompanying pie chart.

Counting the overall defects in the top chart gives us a good idea of how the process is behaving over time. Notice the downward trend from point #8 through point #18. This is a good trend. It's too bad it was not studied to find out what was going so well; the return to a higher number of defects in the last four points might have been avoided.

Our final example of a control chart is also for counted defects. It will be slightly different because we will measure the proportion of total output that was defective. If any of the finished products has any of the possible defects it will be counted as a defective unit (see Figure 9.9).

The proportion of total output that is defective (has one or more defects) each day is plotted from left to right in the upper chart. Notice the upward trend from point #5 through point #12. The control limits are variable because the quantity of total output changes daily.

Over the full period of the study, the defects are categorized to see which problems are most significant. Again, we will add another chart at the bottom. In this case, a Pareto chart is used.

One thing you can see clearly in the top chart that is different from the previous three control charts: the control limits change from point to point. This is a function of the sample size. On data points where the number of items produced is higher, the control limits are closer to the centerline because the sample size is greater. Remember that higher sample sizes lead to increased confidence in our results. Lower sample sizes bring wider control limits.

There is a lot more that can be said about control charts, and there are several more kinds. These basic four will help you produce a control/response plan that is useful and timely, and they can also be used outside the context of a project in ongoing process management.

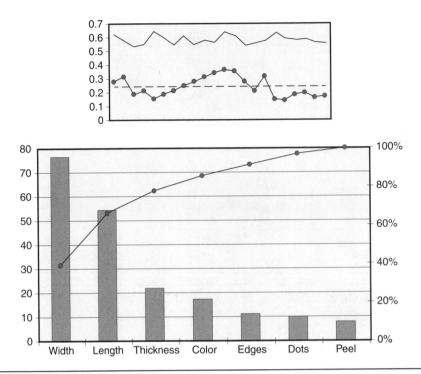

Figure 9.9   Discrete data plotted in p-chart with accompanying Pareto chart.

RANDOM VARIATION AND SPECIAL CAUSE VARIATION

In addition to seeing a point that is outside the control limits, there are other equally important ways to identify nonrandom variation in the process using control charts. *Random variation* will not show a repeating pattern. If there is a display of variation that shows a pattern, this is known as *special cause variation* because there is usually a reason for it, and that reason can be identified, removed, and prevented from occurring in the future.

The key to Six Sigma is to control variation. This is done by removing special cause variation and minimizing random variation.

Some examples of special cause variation that can be identified through the use of control charts are:

- *Shift.* Eight or more points in a row on the same side of the centerline indicate a shift in the process (Figure 9.10). Find out what was different about the process during the shift.

- *Trend.* Seven or more points continuously increasing or decreasing (Figure 9.11). Often seen after some change was made in the process. If you miss a negative

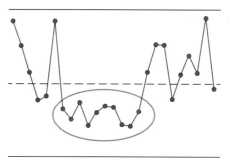

Figure 9.10 Control chart showing shift in the process.

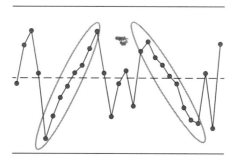

Figure 9.11 Control chart showing positive and negative trends.

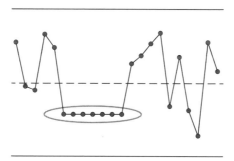

Figure 9.12 Control chart showing "stuck" process.

trend and do not study it, it can happen again. If you watch a positive trend and do not study it, you may not be able to produce it again.

- *Stuck.* Seven or more points in a row having exactly the same value (Figure 9.12). Measurement device may be stuck, or operator may be rounding to the next whole number.

- *Cycle*. Chart shows higher and lower groups of values over equal periods of time (Figure 9.13). Find out what the clusters above and below the center line have in common.

Now our control/response plan will have the charting mechanism listed as well (see Figure 9.14).

As a note, the sections on control charts in this chapter can be useful, and control charts should be used whenever possible, inside or outside the context of an improvement project. If you do not prepare a control chart with centerline and control limits, at least plot your data so everyone can get a quick picture of what is going on in the process. Even if only a time series plot is used to track a continuous output, that will still be useful. If a Pareto or pie chart is used to track categories of defects, that is still going to help you identify problems in the process. The important thing is to track the data, whether or not your chart is perfect.

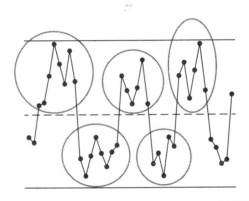

Figure 9.13   Control chart showing cyclical variation.

Process map		Data collection plan	Response plan
Step 1	Notes on step 1	Process variable 1—I-MR chart	
Step 2	Notes on step 2	Process variable 2—p-chart	
Step 3	Notes on step 3		
...	...	Process output—$\bar{X}$ and *s* chart	
Final step	Notes on final step		

Figure 9.14   Control/response plan with tracking mechanism listed in data collection plan section.

RESPONSE PLAN

Okay, we're tracking the progress of our process, and one day something on our chart does not look right. What do we do? This is where the response plan comes into play. The term "response plan" was chosen carefully because a response is planned and executed when it is needed. If we used "reaction plan" instead, it would seem less organized. Our response plan will include instructions on how to handle out-of-control indicators or process breakdowns.

The instructions that someone needs to follow can be as simple or as complex as necessary. Anything from "run two sample tests on four of the last ten pieces of output when any out-of-control indicators are present" to "turn the machine off and call the manager" will give the operator an idea of what steps to take. In either case, and everywhere in between, having the response plan in place is far better than giving the operator no instruction or providing advice during orientation training that might be forgotten before the first out-of-control indicator ever shows up. The objective of the control/response plan is to provide working instructions for how to conduct the process, how to measure it, and how to handle problems that may arise. The finished product depicted in Figure 9.15 will accomplish that objective.

PROJECT CLOSURE

Now you've identified the need for an improvement, scheduled a team to work on it, studied the variables involved in the process, determined those factors that are causing the problem, identified and tested solutions to the problems based on that knowledge, institutionalized the improvements, and completed the project. And it only took the team eighty-nine days to make all of this happen. Congratulations! Now what? Simply put,

Process map		Data collection plan	Response plan
Step 1	Notes on step 1		
Step 2	Notes on step 2	Process variable 1—I-MR chart	For a shift in the data, check with supervisor on material lot
Step 3	Notes on step 3	Process variable 2—p-chart	If defect code CV-1 or CD-3 increases past 1.7%, mark the log and call department manager
...	...	Process output—$\bar{X}$ and s chart	For out-of-control indicators, check with audit staff on QC results for past one hour
Final step	Notes on final step		

Figure 9.15 Completed control/response plan.

celebrate this success, track the savings, and move on to the next project. Your project charter is the first page of the storyboard you may be asked to prepare to summarize your project. Setting up a simple presentation starting with *define* and moving through *measure*, *analyze*, *improve*, and *control*, listing the actions you took and the decisions you made, will help preserve the knowledge gained by your team so it can be used again in another setting. Knowledge management is often overlooked. If a member of the team leaves the organization, don't let that person fail to transfer the valuable knowledge gained during the project.

It is a great achievement to conduct a project that leads to improvements. Each project that you lead can be better than the last one if you take the things you learn from each one and apply them. By identifying improvement opportunities, scoping them clearly, managing good projects in a reasonable period of time (about ninety days), and sustaining the improvements, you will help your organization and showcase your value to the team and its leaders. Congratulations!

Final Team Meeting

Plan a Half Day for the Final Team Meeting

The team will review the pilot test results and make any necessary adjustments. This is important because the final improved process must be implemented as smoothly as possible, so any possible hindrances must be removed, mitigated, or at least brought to the attention of those who will execute the process.

One bad example of implementation is the company that was testing a new software package in one of its fifteen offices. When the test was complete, the testing office sent back a list of 22 bugs they had found in the program. The home office then rolled out the software package to the other fourteen offices with an accompanying note that read, "Watch out for the following 22 problems." Why even bother to test it if you're not going to fix the problems first?!

The team will finalize the control/response plan, including the items shown in Figure 9.15, and prepare the process owners to begin monitoring the process using the prescribed metrics. Failure by the process owners to use the metrics listed in the control/response plan (and only those metrics) will undermine the effectiveness of the improvement project, produce waste in the process, and could lead to a return to the preimprovement state. None of us wants this.

Finally, the team will prepare a communication plan to share the improved process with the organization. They will consider the timing and methods of communication, and will celebrate the success of the team.

Recognition of team members by the project leader, project sponsor, and any other relevant senior leaders should take place here. It was a great project, you got it done in ninety days, and you deserve some praise.

Part VI

Overall Business Process Management

10

Process Management and Lean Thinking

If you've skipped ahead to this chapter, there is no need to go back yet. Whether you've just completed a valuable improvement project in ninety days (congratulations!) or not, this chapter will be useful for you.

OBJECTIVES

We have two objectives for this chapter. To present the first, we have to remember that $y = f(x)$; in other words, variable "y," the output of the process, is created as a result of one or more "x" factors. Growing juicy tomatoes depends on the type of seed, the amount of water and sun, the acidity of the soil, the plant food used, and more "x" variables. In this case, "y" is juiciness. In your process, to produce your desired output, or y, you must prepare the right recipe for your combination of x variables. If you know what x factors will cause your output to be successful, you'll focus squarely on those for maintenance. If you know what x factors will cause your output to fail, you'll focus on those for improvement. And if you know what x factors have no effect at all on your output, you will not waste your time and energy trying to make those factors better. In fact, you may look for ways to eliminate them from the process entirely. *This is our first objective in process management: to control your process actively by managing the important factors and not wasting energy on unimportant ones.* To achieve this goal, you will use the control/response plan and the failure modes and effects analysis.

Objective number two is to use proven skills and techniques to enable your entire team to identify and implement process improvements. To achieve objective #2, you will use a set of tools introduced through lean enterprise, and a few others. Your team will be more powerful when using the materials in this chapter to control, improve, and sustain your excellent processes.

USING DMAIC FOR ONGOING PROCESS MANAGEMENT

You and your team are engaged in a *process*: a series of events that you actively execute in order to transform one or more inputs into an output that is valuable to your customer. You are probably engaged in several processes, some of which are your direct responsibility and some that you support for others. Keeping those processes running smoothly is difficult enough. How are you supposed to make improvements too?

A ninety-day improvement project is possible using the program described in the first nine chapters of this book. It is even more likely that you will be able to identify, study, solve, and control problems when you are managing your processes thoroughly in the first place. What is involved in process management? Some familiar language: *define, measure, analyze, improve,* and *control.*

DEFINE THE PROCESS

The goal for our process is to produce an output that our customer values. The customer has an expectation, and we must live up to that expectation or the customer might start buying from somebody else. The production manager might tell the team in his factory, "Our job is to make good parts only." The call center manager might tell her agents, "Handle every call like it is the most important one of all." Good advice.

As we have discussed earlier, there must be a recognized or documented process in place, and it must be followed by the operators in order for it to be studied and improved. If one person does the job differently each time, or if everyone does the job in a different way than everyone else does it, it will be difficult to meet the customer's needs consistently. And even when we do please the customer, we may not have any idea why we were successful or how we can do it again. For these reasons, the process needs to be documented clearly and enforced.

We covered the steps in process mapping in Chapter 2. Process maps are very useful for a team that is trying to stabilize a process, for use after making an improvement, and especially for new hires. You want your new team members to be successful on their first day, so give them a detailed process map with work instructions and, if necessary, diagrams to follow.

The Value Stream

The input to the process, the steps taken during the process, the suppliers, operators, and customers in the process, and the outputs of the process are elements in a value stream. Implied in the term "value stream" is the customer's willingness to pay for these elements because they are valuable to the customer. If any input, action, output, or other variable in the process is not valuable to the customer, then it should be considered a target for elimination or modification using a tool like the RAMMPP matrix, described later in this chapter.

There are three categories of variables. The two main categories are value-adding (VA), and non-value-adding (NVA). Value-adding steps in the process are those that actually transform the product or deliver the service. Non-value-adding steps reflect the eight wastes of lean, described in Chapter 2, and are steps that do not fit the definition of value-adding. We want to provide through our process only that which is of value to

---

The Paper Airplane Exercise

Split your group into a number of teams, each team having three or four members. Instruct the teams to send one member outside, or into another room. This person is the "tester."

The assignment for the remaining team members is to build a paper airplane that will fly about twelve to fifteen feet and land in a circle that you have taped or marked on the floor. The circle should be about five feet in diameter. Give them a time limit, like ten minutes, to finish.

Once the team has accomplished this task, then the heart of the activity begins. They must now prepare documented instructions for their missing team member to build the same exact design that they made, without showing their airplane to the tester. Give them twenty minutes to prepare instructions.

Invite the testers into the room and show them to their workstations. Don't tell them anything; let the documents prepared by their other team members do the talking.

The testers must build a perfect match to the original plane and also fly the planes they built into the circle. Give them three attempts to hit the circle. You may develop a point scale and award a prize to the winning team, or to all the teams. Points, if awarded, should include both design compliance and hitting the target.

Some teams will write everything on paper, some will include sketches of the folds, and some may use multiple pages of paper to demonstrate each fold, omitting only the last fold based on the instruction not to show the tester the finished plane.

After all planes have been flown, debrief the full group on the effectiveness of their instructions. Ask the group, "If this were a new employee and this were their first day on the job, could he or she have been successful using the documented instructions?"

We want work instructions that are so complete and easy to understand that someone can be successful the first day on the job.

---

our customer, and any other things should be removed in order to save money, avoid mistakes, and get the process accomplished more quickly. A good exercise to identify which of the two categories each variable in our process falls into is to ask, for each one, "If we stopped doing this, would our customers care?"

Before doing this exercise, it is useful to discuss the third category, the operational, or value-enabling (VE), variable. This is an input, action step, or output that is necessary for the continuation of our work, even if it does not add value for our customer. An example of a VE step would be regulatory reporting, which is not usually important to the customer yet very important to the organization.

When our process is defined, and everyone has agreed that this is the way we will do business, it must be documented and posted for everyone's use. It must be enforced in its application every time. And it must be measured for accuracy and control.

Inspection Does Not Make a Process Work Better

One additional thing is true about either a VA or VE process: it is only adding value if it is done correctly the first time. When a mistake is made and you have to do something—anything—for a second time, time is wasted and money is wasted.

Sure, if you are able to uncover a mistake the moment it is made and correct it on the spot, less time and money are being lost. If you have inspection steps built into the process down the line and you uncover problems at that point, then you have to go back to the place where the problem was created and fix it, or fix it during inspection. That is more costly in time and money than instant correction. And the worst case is when you did not uncover the problem inside your own building, and the product or service was delivered to the customer, and only then was the problem identified. That late discovery costs you time, money, and a possible customer relationship.

This is where the detectability score in the FMEA presented in Chapter 7 is so useful. Taking the time now to think about how quickly you can determine that an error has been made will save you time and money right away.

Also, a word on inspections and quality control: They are, as defined in lean thinking, waste. No change of the product takes place, the customer is not willing to pay for your internal inspection, and you are paying somebody or buying some machine that is used only to detect whether something was done incorrectly in your process. I'm not suggesting that you eliminate inspection or QC today before you've improved and error-proofed your processes. I would, however, ask if you could calculate how much time and money you would save if your process steps were being executed correctly the first time, every time, and you did not need to conduct inspections at all.

MEASURE THE PROCESS

The control/response plan created in Chapter 9 is a visual tool that lists the appropriate ongoing measures to track in your process. If you look at the output of your process as a variable named y, and all the other variables that go into your process and take place within the process as variables named x_1, x_2, x_3, and so on, then y is a function of the x variables, or a result of the combination of all those x's. The mathematical notation would be: $y = f(x_1, x_2, x_3, ..., x_n)$.

Some of those x variables will have more of an impact on the y than others, and you will figure those out during the analyze phase of an improvement project. You also may already know which x's are more important in your process because of previous improvement efforts you have conducted. These are the x variables that need to be measured on an ongoing basis. If you are only measuring your output, or y, then you will miss the opportunity to make improvements before the finished product is made. Tracking variables during the process helps you to avoid problems before they reach your customer.

It is also a very good idea to conduct a measurement system analysis on all the important metrics in your organization. If one person measures one thing two or three times and gets different results, that is an inconsistent measurement system, and it needs to be improved or else you will have difficulty in tracking the capability of your process. Also, if two or more people measure the same thing and get different results, this is also a great opportunity to cause problems. It is especially true if you are measuring the output of your process one way and your customer is measuring it differently. An example discussed previously is the air pressure used to test a pop-off valve: the manufacturer used 3 psi and the customer used 5 psi. The manufacturer found zero defects and the customer found 30% defective!

In another previous example, a call center was having trouble with employee attrition. Large numbers of people were quitting their jobs, and no real improvement had been made in over two years. Instead of jumping to conclusions, the new manager started by looking at exit interview data. What she found was a difference in the classification of reasons people left the company. One person who left for a different job in the same city could be classified by one interviewer as "better opportunity," while another interviewer might use "more pay" for the same circumstances. The manager and the HR team collaborated on a revised and shorter list of categories so they could really identify the reasons people were leaving their jobs and then develop plans to combat those issues. They then tested all the interviewers to calibrate the selection of reason codes so that everyone would evaluate the same situation the same way every time.

ANALYZE THE PROCESS

Several very good tools for analyzing your process have already been mentioned. Let's look at a few more that you can use any time.

A very useful tool that was popularized by General Electric through its Workout program is the RAMMPP Matrix (RAMMPP is an acronym referring to the items listed down the left-hand side of Figure 10.1). When used by a team to evaluate its processes, the RAMMPP matrix will help us eliminate waste in our processes.

For a RAMMPP session you will ask the participants to bring with them their list of all the things in the left-hand column that they own, do, contribute to, receive, read, discard, or that affect or involve them in any way. All those items will be listed in the matrix

	Self	Department	Group	Company	External
Reports					
Approvals					
Meetings					
Measures					
Policies					
Practices					

Figure 10.1   RAMMPP matrix.

in the appropriate box based on what type of thing it is (report, approval, meeting, and so on) and who has control over that item (self, department manager, other group leader, the whole company, or an external customer, supplier, or authority).

Now comes the fun part. For each item listed on the matrix, the team will be asked the following questions until the answer to at least one of them is "Yes":

- Could it be eliminated entirely?

- Could part of it be eliminated to save time or energy?

- Could it be delegated?

- Could it be done less often?

- Could it be simplified?

- Could it be done in less time?

- Could it be done using a more productive technology?

- Is there something else we can do with this to make it easier or less time-consuming?

This is a tool that can be used at any time by any group of people. So many things build up over time that could be eliminated or simplified. Reports or approvals that were originally created in response to a temporary problem have now become permanent procedures. Metrics are tracked for variables that are not important for our process. You may have outdated practices in the workplace that were based on previous technology, and outdated policies that have outlived their usefulness and are no longer appropriate. And meetings—oh, so many meetings. Meetings that are unproductive, recurring meetings that everyone attends out of habit, and meetings where critical participants are absent—all are a drain on time and energy, and a high cost for any organization.

Analyzing your process on an ongoing basis will help you uncover issues early, before they reach your customer, and will give you great ideas for improvement projects that can be executed in ninety days.

IMPROVE THE PROCESS

Before introducing the topic of improvement, I'd like to point out the two types of mistakes that can be made in identifying problems and targeting them for improvement. The first is when you conduct analysis on the process and identify a problem *that is not really a significant issue*. This can result from analysis that is conducted hastily or incorrectly, from not having the right team assembled, or from someone's gut feeling or suspicion about the root cause. When you attempt to correct a problem that is really not affecting your process outcome, this is known as *tampering*, and it can cause delay and, at its worst, will make a process worse than it was.

The second type of mistake in problem identification is a *missed signal*. This is the opposite of the first type: you do not attempt to fix an issue that really is a significant cause of the problems in your process. A possible root cause from your fishbone diagram may be seen by the team or its manager as not being important and disregarded, yet a thorough analysis would have shown that it really is significant. Don't rule out a possibility until it is validated.

How to Improve the Process

Process improvement begins with each person who will participate in continuous improvement, and the first step each person and each department should take is 5S. Before a continuous improvement program can be successful, the members of the team need to see the value in it. Making change can often be difficult, and process excellence requires change, so such a program may be unwelcome. To build a culture of improvement, you'll start at the ground level and then add blocks and layers. As in building a mighty pyramid, you will need a strong foundation in order to provide stability for the upward construction and to withstand any resistance you may face.

If you picture a small factory with individual workstations that are grouped into departments, those individual workstations need to be working as efficiently as possible before a larger project to improve performance of an entire department can be successful. If one moving part is not oiled, it will slow down the whole machine.

For example, in a law firm these workstations are the individual attorneys and the individual legal secretaries (see Figure 10.2). Before you can make a good, lasting process improvement in a practice group or department, each person needs to be working as smoothly as possible.

Now, I know it can be difficult to suggest that a specific attorney could be working more efficiently! What I'd like to recommend is that you offer advice that has been proven in many settings, and it is this: 5S is easy, and you can start making really useful improvements today.

What is 5S in practical terms? It is a series of steps that will make an individual work space more productive with very little effort. Let's look at what each step means briefly:

- *Sort.* The first step: eliminate anything that is unnecessary or has not been used for a period of time, like one year. Keep only things that are important and

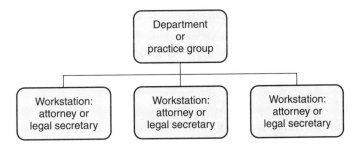

Figure 10.2   "Workstations" in a law firm.

useful. For those items that are being kept because maybe, someday, I might need it, put them in a location farther away from your work space so they do not get in the way of your productivity.

- *Set in order.* Keep everything where it belongs and return things—yours and others'—to where you found them. When something arrives in your work space, you are able to determine *with one touch* where you need to put it and what you need to do with it.

- *Shine.* Keep your area clean so that clutter and even dust, which can be obstacles to productivity, are removed and kept away from your work space.

- *Standardize.* To be able to handle each new arriving piece of work or information with one touch, you must develop a recurring process for handling them. Follow your practices consistently so that there is no mystery when sorting and setting your work in order.

- *Sustain.* Develop a regular pattern of doing the first four S's and sharing your practices with others who work in a similar setting. Track and monitor each other's progress and make sure everyone is continuing to follow 5S.

With a 5S program in place, you'll have a foundation from which to launch improvement projects that will be more successful than they'd be without this formative level of individual excellence and discipline. So, how do you start?

Try this exercise yourself, and then share it with your team members: At the end of each day, put your wastebasket on your chair. From a standing position, pick up everything on your desk one item at a time and, with only one touch, find the right place for it. It may need to be filed, it may need to be sent to somebody else, it may need to be put back in your in-box for you to handle the next day, or it may need to be pitched into the trash. Don't leave until everything is in its place. *This exercise will get easier every day!*

The SCAMPER Technique

Outside the context of an improvement project, there are other tools that you and your team can use to make improvements at any time. Another popular and effective tool is the *SCAMPER technique*. It is a quick and logical exercise that can be done individually or in a group, and its purpose is to give you a different view of your process than the way you see it every day.

List the steps in your process in order and all the variables (materials, machines, metrics, environment, methods, and people) that are involved in the process. Then ask, for each item, the following series of questions:

S—Can I *substitute* something? Can I use an alternate material, another team member, or a different ingredient? What can I substitute to save time, energy, and cost?

C—What can I *combine*? Can I combine steps, approvals, meetings, or reports? What can I combine to reduce time, energy, and cost?

A—What can I *adapt*? Is there something being done by somebody else that I can apply to my process? Who can I ask?

M—Can I *modify, magnify,* or *minimize* some aspect of my process to save time, energy, and cost? If I can change something, will it help me save?

P—Can I *put* something that is working well to another use? If I have a good practice in one area, can I use it somewhere else or share that idea with somebody else?

E—What can I *eliminate* from my process entirely? If there is no need to use it, do it, send it, write it, or otherwise keep it going, will it save time, energy, and cost if I stop?

R—What can I *rearrange* in my process? If I change the order of my process or an adjacent process (following my spaghetti diagram), will I save time, energy, or cost?

The SCAMPER technique is a great way to look at your process at any time (like every Monday or the first of each month) because requirements change frequently, and it is usually the case that more requirements are added than are removed. Take the time to improve your process locally and you'll have more time for your other assignments and your other improvement projects.

CONTROL THE PROCESS

A few words on controlling your improved process: The primary tool to use is the control/response plan, detailed in Chapter 9 of this book. It is a great idea to put a control/response plan in place for all your processes so that everyone will know what is expected, even those who are just starting the job. If that sounds like a big job, just start with one process and build momentum throughout the organization. When you've finished with one process, move to the next and keep going.

CLOSING THOUGHTS

1. The most important thing about process control is to live it every day. If you walk away from reading this book saying, "This stuff will not work for me," then it will not work for you. The ancient Chinese proverb reads: "The best time to plant a tree is twenty years ago. The next best time is right now." By reading this material you have taken a very big step toward process control, which means meeting your customer's expectations, and doing it efficiently. If

it is important enough to *start* making these improvements, then it is important enough to *stay dedicated* to that pursuit all the time.

2.   To preserve the knowledge gained through Six Sigma improvement projects, local improvements, good practices, and usage of good tools and techniques, your organization would be well served by a knowledge management program. Whether it includes a mentoring program, an FAQ section on your intranet, or a more formal set of current and historical documents, being able to capture knowledge, analyze its usefulness, and distribute it where it is needed will save time in all areas and functions throughout the year.

3.   Celebrate success! When a team or individual has made a good improvement, take a minute to make it known that you appreciate the work and to let others know that there are improvements being made in your organization. This will also serve to improve your knowledge management program, and to show that you and others are living this cultural change every day. And, especially when an improvement project has been completed with sustainable and demonstrable benefits in a ninety-day time period, that is truly something that calls for celebration!

Glossary

activity-based costing—An accounting system that assigns costs to a product based on the amount of resources used to design, order, or make it.

analysis of variance (ANOVA)—A basic statistical technique for determining the proportion of influence a factor or set of factors has on total variation. It subdivides the total variation of a data set into meaningful component parts associated with specific sources of variation to test a hypothesis on the parameters of the model or to estimate variance components. There are three models: fixed, random, and mixed.

Black Belt (BB)—Full-time team leader responsible for implementing process improvement projects—define, measure, analyze, improve, and control (DMAIC) or define, measure, analyze, design, and verify (DMADV)—within a business to drive up customer satisfaction and productivity levels.

brainstorming—A technique teams use to generate ideas on a particular subject. Each person on the team is asked to think creatively and write down as many ideas as possible. The ideas are not discussed or reviewed until after the brainstorming session.

cause-and-effect diagram—*See* fishbone diagram.

centerline—A line on a graph that represents the overall average (mean) operating level of the process.

charter—A written commitment approved by management stating the scope of authority for an improvement project or team.

check sheet—A simple data recording device. The check sheet is custom-designed by the user, which allows him or her to readily interpret the results.

common causes—Causes of variation that are inherent in a process over time. They affect every outcome of the process and everyone working in the process. *See also* special causes.

consultant—An individual who has experience and expertise in applying tools and techniques to resolve process problems and who can advise and facilitate an organization's improvement efforts.

continuous improvement (CI)—The ongoing improvement of products, services, or processes through incremental and breakthrough improvements.

control chart—A chart with upper and lower control limits on which values of some statistical measure for a series of samples or subgroups are plotted. The chart frequently shows a central line to help detect a trend of plotted values toward either control limit.

control limits—The natural boundaries of a process within specified confidence levels, expressed as the upper control limit (UCL) and the lower control limit (LCL).

critical processes—Processes that present serious potential dangers to human life, health, and the environment, or that risk the loss of significant sums of money or customers.

cross-functional—A term used to describe a process or an activity that crosses the boundary between functions. A cross-functional team consists of individuals from more than one organizational unit or function.

cycle time—The time required to complete one cycle of an operation. If cycle time for every operation in a complete process can be reduced to equal takt time, products can be made in single-piece flow.

defect—A product's or service's nonfulfillment of an intended requirement or reasonable expectation for use, including safety considerations.

defective—A defective unit; a unit of product that contains one or more defects with respect to the quality characteristic(s) under consideration.

DMAIC—A data-driven quality strategy for improving processes, and an integral part of a Six Sigma quality initiative. DMAIC is an acronym for define, measure, analyze, improve, and control.

effectiveness—The state of having produced a decided-on or desired effect.

efficiency—The ratio of the output to the total input in a process.

efficient—A term describing a process that operates effectively while consuming minimal resources (such as labor and time).

electric data interchange (EDI)—The electronic exchange of data from customers to suppliers and from suppliers to customers.

error-proofing—Use of process or design features to prevent the acceptance or further processing of nonconforming products. Also known as *mistake-proofing*.

facilitator—A specifically trained person who functions as a teacher, coach, and moderator for a group, team, or organization.

failure modes and effects analysis (FMEA)—A systematized group of activities to recognize and evaluate the potential failure of a product or process and its effects, identify actions that could eliminate or reduce the occurrence of the potential failure, and document the process.

fishbone diagram— A diagram illustrating the main causes and subcauses leading to an effect (symptom), so named because it resembles a fish skeleton. It is also referred to as the *Ishikawa diagram* because Kaoru Ishikawa developed it.

five S's (5S)—Five Japanese terms beginning with "s" used to create a workplace suited for visual control and lean production.

five whys—A technique for discovering the root causes of a problem and showing the relationship of causes by repeatedly asking the question, "why?"

flow—The progressive achievement of tasks along the value stream so a product proceeds from design to launch, order to delivery, and raw to finished materials in the hands of the customer with no stoppages, scrap, or backflows.

flowchart—A graphical representation of the steps in a process. Flowcharts are drawn to better understand processes.

gage repeatability and reproducibility (GR&R)—The evaluation of a gauging instrument's accuracy by determining whether its measurements are repeatable (there is close agreement between a number of consecutive measurements of the output for the same value of the input under the same operating conditions) and reproducible (there is close agreement between repeated measurements of the output for the same value of input made under the same operating conditions over a period of time).

Green Belt (GB)—An employee who has been trained in the Six Sigma improvement method and will lead a process improvement or quality improvement team as part of his or her full-time job.

inputs—The products, services, and material obtained from suppliers to produce the outputs delivered to customers.

inspection—Measuring, examining, testing, and gauging one or more characteristics of a product or service and comparing the results with specified requirements to determine whether conformity is achieved for each characteristic.

Ishikawa diagram—*See* fishbone diagram.

kaizen—A Japanese term that means gradual unending improvement by doing little things better and setting and achieving increasingly higher standards.

lean manufacturing/production—An initiative focused on eliminating all waste in manufacturing processes. Principles of lean manufacturing include zero waiting time, zero inventory, scheduling (internal customer pull instead of push system), batch to flow (cut batch sizes), line balancing, and cutting actual process times.

Master Black Belt (MBB)—Six Sigma or quality expert responsible for strategic implementations in an organization. An MBB is qualified to teach other Six Sigma facilitators the methods, tools, and applications in all functions and levels of the company and is a resource for using statistical process control in processes.

mean—A measure of central tendency; the arithmetic average of all measurements in a data set.

measurement system—All operations, procedures, devices, and other equipment or personnel used to assign a value to the characteristic being measured.

median—The middle number or center value of a set of data in which all the data are arranged in sequence.

n—The number of units in a sample.

non-value-added—A term that describes a process step or function that is not required for the direct achievement of process output. This step or function is identified and examined for potential elimination.

out-of-control process—A process in which the statistical measure being evaluated is not in a state of statistical control. In other words, the variations between the observed sampling results can be attributed to a constant system of chance causes.

Pareto chart—A graphical tool for ranking causes from most significant to least significant, most frequently occurring to least, most costly to least costly, or other sorting criteria.

process—A set of interrelated work activities characterized by a set of specific inputs and value-added tasks that make up a procedure for producing a set of specific outputs.

process management—The pertinent techniques and tools applied to a process to implement and improve process effectiveness, hold the gains, and ensure process integrity in fulfilling customer requirements.

process map—A type of flowchart depicting the steps in a process and identifying responsibility for each step and key measures.

process owner—The person who coordinates the various functions and work activities at all levels of a process, has the authority or ability to make changes in the process as required, and manages the entire process cycle to ensure performance effectiveness.

productivity—A measurement of output for a given amount of input.

project team—A group that manages the work of a project. The work typically involves balancing competing demands for project scope, time, cost, risk, and quality, satisfying stakeholders with differing needs and expectations, and meeting identified requirements.

quality control—The operational techniques and activities used to fulfill requirements for quality. Often embodied in postproduction inspection steps.

random cause—A cause of variation due to chance and not assignable to any factor. *See also* common causes.

random sampling—A commonly used sampling technique in which sample units are selected so all combinations of *n* units under consideration have an equal chance of being selected as the sample.

regression analysis—A statistical technique for determining the best mathematical expression describing the functional relationship between one response and one or more independent variables.

repeatability—The variation in measurements obtained when one measurement device is used several times by the same person to measure the same characteristic on the same product.

reproducibility—The variation in measurements made by different people using the same measuring device to measure the same characteristic on the same product.

scatter diagram—A graphical technique for analyzing the relationship between two variables. Two sets of data are plotted on a graph, with the *y*-axis being the variable to be predicted and the *x*-axis being the variable that will be used to make the prediction.

SIPOC diagram—A tool used by Six Sigma process improvement teams to identify all relevant elements (suppliers, inputs, processes, outputs, customers) of a process improvement project before work begins.

Six Sigma—A method that provides organizations with tools to improve the capability of their business processes. This increase in performance and decrease in process variation leads to defect reduction and improvement in profits, employee morale, and quality of products or services.

special causes—Causes of variation that arise because of special circumstances. They are not an inherent part of a process.

tampering—Action taken to compensate for variation that is within the control limits of a stable system, in other words, treating random variation as if there were a special cause; tampering actually increases rather than decreases variation.

T-test—A testing method used to assess whether the means of two groups are statistically different from each other.

value analysis—Analyzing the value stream to identify value-added and non-value-added activities.

value stream—All activities, both value-added and non-value-added, required to bring a product from raw material state into the hands of the customer, bring a customer requirement from order to delivery, and bring a design from concept to launch.

value stream mapping—A pencil and paper tool used in two stages. First, follow a product's production path from beginning to end and draw a visual representation of every process in the material and information flows. Second, draw a future state map of how value should flow. The most important map is the future state map.

value-added—A term used to describe activities that transform input into a customer (internal or external)–usable output.

waste—Any activity that consumes resources and produces no added value to the product or service a customer receives.

Index

A

accuracy
  in measurement, 47
  in process problems, 5
  speed, and cost, conflicts between, 4, 92
activities, under activity-based costing, 97
activity-based costing (ABC), 96–98
  similarity to Lean Six Sigma, 98
activity-based management, 96
alternate hypothesis, 74
analyze, phase of DMAIC methodology, 55–79
  in ongoing process management, 121–22
ANOVA (analysis of variance), 71–73
"as is" process map, 102

B

bias, in sampling, 34
Black Belts, Six Sigma
  role in improvement projects, xvii
  role in project coaching, 78
box and whisker plot, 67
box plot, 67
business case, in project charter, 9–10
business problem, translating into statistical
    problem, 69–70
business process management, 115–26
business solution, translating statistical solution
    into, 77–78

C

cause-and-effect chart, 57–60
causes, of problems, identifying, 57–68
c-chart, 108–9
communication plan, 114
consistent measurement, 47–53
  principles of, 47–49
continuous input, 76–77
continuous measures (data), 71, 78

control charts for, 105–8
continuous variable
  sample size calculation with, 39
  in statistical hypothesis testing, 71, 72
control, phase of DMAIC methodology, 99–114
  in ongoing process management, 125
control charts, 104–9
control limits, 105–6
control/response plan, 101–14
  in ongoing process management, 125
cost
  accuracy, and speed, conflicts between, 4, 92
  in process problems, 5
cost driver, under activity-based costing, 97
cost/benefit analysis, 95–98
  template, 95–96
customers, in SIPOC chart, 14
cycle, in control chart data, 112
cyclical variation, 68, 112

D

data
  collecting sufficient, 31–46
  graphing, 63–68
data collection
  for control/response plan, 102–4
  during improvement project, 42–43, 54
  rules for, 43–44
  three phases of, 41–46
data collection plan, 41, 42, 43, 54
defect rate
  and sample size, 37–38
  and sigma value, 42
defects
  categories of, in root cause analysis, 58–59
  as waste, 25
defects per million opportunities (DPMO), 42
define, phase of DMAIC methodology, 1–32
  in ongoing process management, 118–19
Deming, W. Edwards, 59
design FMEA, 84

Belong to the Quality Community!

Established in 1946, ASQ is a global community of quality experts in all fields and industries. ASQ is dedicated to the promotion and advancement of quality tools, principles, and practices in the workplace and in the community.

The Society also serves as an advocate for quality. Its members have informed and advised the U.S. Congress, government agencies, state legislatures, and other groups and individuals worldwide on quality-related topics.

Vision

By making quality a global priority, an organizational imperative, and a personal ethic, ASQ becomes the community of choice for everyone who seeks quality technology, concepts, or tools to improve themselves and their world.

ASQ is...

- More than 90,000 individuals and 700 companies in more than 100 countries

- The world's largest organization dedicated to promoting quality

- A community of professionals striving to bring quality to their work and their lives

- The administrator of the Malcolm Baldrige National Quality Award

- A supporter of quality in all sectors including manufacturing, service, healthcare, government, and education

- YOU

Visit www.asq.org for more information.

ASQ

ASQ Membership

Research shows that people who join associations experience increased job satisfaction, earn more, and are generally happier*. ASQ membership can help you achieve this while providing the tools you need to be successful in your industry and to distinguish yourself from your competition. So why wouldn't you want to be a part of ASQ?

Networking

Have the opportunity to meet, communicate, and collaborate with your peers within the quality community through conferences and local ASQ section meetings, ASQ forums or divisions, ASQ Communities of Quality discussion boards, and more.

Professional Development

Access a wide variety of professional development tools such as books, training, and certifications at a discounted price. Also, ASQ certifications and the ASQ Career Center help enhance your quality knowledge and take your career to the next level.

Solutions

Find answers to all your quality problems, big and small, with ASQ's Knowledge Center, mentoring program, various e-newsletters, *Quality Progress* magazine, and industry-specific products.

Access to Information

Learn classic and current quality principles and theories in ASQ's Quality Information Center (QIC), *ASQ Weekly* e-newsletter, and product offerings.

Advocacy Programs

ASQ helps create a better community, government, and world through initiatives that include social responsibility, Washington advocacy, and Community Good Works.

Visit www.asq.org/membership for more information on ASQ membership.

*2008, The William E. Smith Institute for Association Research